SONS OF STRUTH DEMAND THE TRUTH

THE INSIDE STORY OF THE BATTLE FOR POWER AT RANGERS

To Colin

Follow Follow

[signature]
SOS

CRAIG HOUSTON

First published 2015
By M.M.M.&C.

Copyright ©Craig Houston 2015

A CIP catalogue record for this title is available from the British Library

ISBN 978-0-9935126-0-5

Printed and Bound by MBM Print SCS Ltd, Glasgow

FOR BEN AND AMY
AND
FOR MY DAD
ROBERT HOUSTON
(1944 – 2015)

CONTENTS

FOREWORD
BY JOHN BROWN

I worked as a first team scout for Rangers during Craig Whyte's tenure at the Ibrox club.

But it was very difficult. In fact, it was a mess from day one. No guidance was ever given about the level of player the club could afford. Fundamentals, like new player salaries and transfer budgets, weren't discussed so targeting potential signings was virtually impossible.

When Whyte placed Rangers into administration in 2012, and Charles Green subsequently arrived as the figurehead of a consortium which was intent on buying the club and had soon been handed preferred bidder status any hope of matters improving was soon extinguished.

At a meeting I attended along with representatives of the Rangers Fans Fighting Fund Committee, Green purported to be monitoring 27 world class players with the intention signing some of them.

But the scouting staff had already appraised the list of players and immediately discounted them on the grounds that the club couldn't afford the huge sums of money they would demand. To suggest any of them would be arriving at Ibrox was pure fantasy. However, I kept my opinions to myself because I was afraid of jeopardising my job.

I was soon approached by a group of businessmen who had very reliable information that, should the Green consortium's bid be successful, the outcome for Rangers Football Club would be disastrous.

These businessman had believed that Rangers were heading for administration a long time before it actually happened. They were of the opinion that it was always the end goal of those heading Rangers at that time.

My contacts were in the process of putting together a bid for Rangers themselves and invited me to advise them on football matters. Around this time, suspicion about Charles Green's close association with Craig Whyte was rife. At a meeting which I attended in London I was warned they would bleed the club dry.

I made my feelings on the situation at Rangers public and Green summoned me to his office. He told me that he could put Rangers out of business whenever he chose. At that exact moment I knew my time as an employee of my boyhood club was over. I refused to be any part of what I suspected lay ahead.

I drove straight to Murray Park, cleared out my office and resigned. I only stopped to call the manager, my old Nine-In-A-Row team mate Ally McCoist, to tell him what I had done and inform him that my fight for the survival of Rangers would continue from the outside.

I had enjoyed many successes during my time at Rangers. I had won leagues and cups, I had scored against Celtic in an Old Firm game and I had represented the club in Europe. So I definitely left with a heavy heart.

But, on reflection, I think departing was the greatest thing I ever did for Rangers. It allowed me to speak freely about the incumbent regime and their intentions.

When I stood on the steps of Ibrox to tell the fans what was happening to their club I was ridiculed, but I felt, and I still do, the fans needed to know what was going on. People started asking if I had "lost the plot". But I needed to do something. No one else was doing a thing. My reputation was left in tatters, but I honestly didn't care.

Sadly, my warnings of impending financial ruin at the club fell on deaf ears. I told of the millions of pounds seeping out of the club but few people believed me.

Fortunately, Craig Houston, who had been monitoring the goings on at Rangers closely for some time, became active in his pursuit of a better way forward for the club. He formed Sons Of Struth with his friend Sandy Chugg and was relentless in his attempts to rid Rangers of the corruption and mismanagement.

His message of "enough is enough" soon started to get through to individual fans and supporters groups alike. Like me, Craig was subjected to threats and abuse, but he carried on, even when his livelihood was at risk. He organised protests on match days, set up displays of red and blue cards during games, arranged marches on the stadium and encouraged countless fans to sign petitions calling for change at the club.

Craig is a very loyal guy. He told me he was 100% behind me and my message and I in turn wanted to do anything and everything I could to help him.

At times, trying to get the fans on board was tough. In spite of many supporters being businessmen and highly-qualified professionals who frequented the hospitality areas at Ibrox they were collectively reluctant to show backing for the fans groups trying to force change.

I am disappointed that, to this day, many of these 'big hitters' chose to stay silent. Perhaps they were worried about the possible effect on them if they spoke up. But they must have known what was going on at Rangers.

Craig is at heart a Rangers man through and through, a working class guy who would do anything for his beloved club. By calling his group Sons of Struth after the legendary former manager Bill Struth he wanted to remind the fans of the fundamental values of our club. Many of the traditions created by Struth are still evident at the club today.

It hasn't been easy for Craig. Many tried to derail his goal and discredit his intentions. But he remained strong. Even when others floundered and followed like sheep, Craig refused to accept anybody or anything that could destroy the future of Rangers Football Club. His is an amazing story. I take my hat off to him.

CHAPTER 1

MR HOLMES?

"You brought Graeme Souness to Rangers. Thank you."

Craig Houston, Rangers supporter, aged 14.

MY old gran, God rest her, had asbestos hands.

Like so many Scottish women of her generation, she had stayed at home and raised her family, my father and his two brothers and sister, while her husband had gone out and earned a wage to put food on the table and pay the bills.

But during the Second World War she had served in the Central Hotel, at the front of the train station of the same name in the city centre of Glasgow, on the waitressing staff and in the kitchens. She had asbestos hands as a result.

I have many happy memories of spending time with my gran in her house in Crookston when I was a young boy growing up. I would go there a great deal with my older sister Fiona during the school holidays.

She would sometimes bake us Empire biscuits - and take the tray they were on out to cool with her bare hands when they were done. As a wee lad, I was just fascinated by this, at how her long bony fingers didn't get burned when she put them in the roasting hot oven. I would watch her transfixed.

Rangers was always going to be the club I followed. My grandfather was a fan and my father was as well. So it was always likely I would end up sharing their allegiance to the Ibrox club. But my gran was every bit as passionate, possibly more so, as her husband and her son. She was probably the biggest influence on the football team I supported.

She had kept programmes of many of the Rangers games she had been to over the years. Every so often she would take them out for me to look through when I was visiting. She would talk in reverential tones about players I had never heard of and regale me with stories of all the many memorable matches she had been to in her life.

The European Cup Winners' Cup final in 1972 had been one of them. My gran and granfather had been at the Nou Camp in Barcelona when Rangers had beaten Moscow Dynamo 3-2 to win their only European trophy.

My family has been represented at every European final Rangers have played in. My grandfather was at both legs of the European Cup Winners' Cup final against Fiorentina in Glasgow and Florence in 1961. My grandfather and my uncle were at the European Cup Winners' Cup final against Bayern Munich in Nuremberg in 1967. My gran and my grandfather were at the European Cup Winners' Cup final at Moscow Dynamo in Barcelona in 1972. And I was at the UEFA Cup final with Zenit St. Petersburg in Manchester in 2008. We will be by no means unique in that distinction among Rangers fans.

When I was old enough, around eight or so, my gran and I started to go to Rangers matches together at Ibrox. She would always take her flask of tea, her packet of sandwiches and a baffling array of other accoutrements along with her.

Her favourite player was Davie Cooper. She just adored him. There was an old boy who used to sit near us at games at that time and if Coops misplaced just one pass or failed to control just one ball he would give him terrible stick. My gran would mutter under her breath when he did so. On the odd occasion, when his abuse got particularly bad and she could bear to listen no longer, she would stand up and put him firmly in his place.

I loved Cooper too. My own favourite memory of the winger was of the free-kick he scored in the famous League Cup final win over Aberdeen at Hampden in 1987. There was so much power in his shot. It hurtled past the opposition goalkeeper Jim Leighton and into the top corner of the net. Even watching it back in slow motion afterwards it was fast.

Legend has it the next time Cooper met Leighton, when they got together with the Scotland squad, his opponent claimed he came close to denying him.

He said to him: "I nearly got to that!"

The story goes that Cooper replied:"Aye, on the way out the ground!"

He died the day before my birthday on March 23, 1995, aged just 39. I was devastated. I idolised him. As did my gran.

For some reason, I was always quite taken by the older members of the Rangers team when I first started going to games. Perhaps it was because of all the stories I had been told by my gran about the successes they had enjoyed in years gone by. I definitely liked the players who were approaching the end of their careers at that time. The likes of Colin Jackson, Sandy Jardine and Tommy McLean stuck out for me. I can also remember being a little bit intimidated by Tam Forsyth.

Later on, John MacDonald became a hero of mine. One of the great thrills of my childhood was meeting him. I was close friends with two brothers called Scott and Stewart Campbell in Linwood. Their mother Betty knew John's mother-in-law. One day, totally out of the blue, we got told we were going to meet him.

He was a first team regular at the time and so we were understandably all excited. He duly appeared at Scott and Stewart's house in his car and drove all three of us up to his mother-in-law's house. We all thought it was pretty spectacular. It was the first time any of us had met a Rangers player.

John was very good at winning penalty kicks. Rangers had played Aberdeen at Ibrox the Saturday before we met him and had been denied what we all thought, from our impartial viewpoint, was a certain spot kick. Alex McLeish had taken him out with what looked more like a rugby tackle than a football tackle to us.

I asked him:"Was that a penalty on Saturday, John?" He just lifted up his shirt. He had a scratch mark from his shoulder right down to his waist where McLeish had hauled him down. He signed autographs and must have spent a couple of hours chatting to us. After that, he became my firm favourite.

My match day routine was always the same at that time. I would play football in the morning, rush home, jump in the shower, throw on my jeans, my Rangers strip and my tracksuit top. Then I would get in the car and my dad would drive down to the Neptune Masonic Lodge just behind the Swallow Hotel on Paisley Road West. I would get put away from the bar in the Master's Room with some toys to play with and some books to read while my dad would have a quick pint. Then we would walk down to the game.

I am the only man in the Houston family for several generations who hasn't been a Master of the Masonic Lodge. My father and my grandfather both were. I can still recall my dad heading out to meetings and social functions at the Neptune wearing his dinner suits, dickie bows and white gloves and carrying a brown briefcase with his apron inside. I've been encouraged to join in the past. But it's not something that's ever really interested me.

As I got older, I started going to Rangers games at Ibrox by myself. Before long I was going to away games as well. I would travel to them on a supporters' bus which left from Linwood or from nearby Johnstone. I was looked after by the older supporters on those trips. But I'm not sure they did a particularly good job of it.

I can still recall one trip to Aberdeen vividly. I was informed we were going to a pub and was told to try and look older. It actually turned out to be a strip club. At one point in proceedings, we all had to throw our Rangers scarves on stage because the lassie was going to come out with them wrapped around her. That was the last I ever saw of my Rangers 1978 Treble Winners scarf.

After Graeme Souness took over as Rangers manager in 1986 things changed for the better at Ibrox. His arrival heralded the dawn of a new era. He was given money to spend and brought in some superb players, not least the England captain Terry Butcher and the England goalkeeper Chris Woods. Clubs down south being banned from European competition for five years by UEFA in the wake of the Heysel Disaster of 1985 also helped to lure such big names to Scotland.

I can remember watching television one night and Butcher was being interviewed. My gran shouted out: "That's that boy we met in Portugal!" My grandparents had been staying at the same hotel as Ipswich Town, where Butcher played for many years, on their holiday. They bumped into him and, even though it was years before he signed for Rangers, had a long chat with him about the Ibrox club. It turned out that John Wark, the Scotland midfielder, was always banging on to the Ipswich team about the team he grew up supporting in Glasgow and they became fans too.

We would go on to dominate Scottish football domestically for some time after that. I always felt that success we enjoyed under Souness, and then Walter Smith after him, was payback for all of the defeats and all the drudgery which I had been subjected to growing up. More and more money was spent and more and more great players arrived.

My favourite Rangers game from that time, and still one of my all-time favourite games to this day, was the 5-1 victory over Celtic at Ibrox in the first Old Firm game of the 1988/89 season. Celtic, who had won the league and cup double in the previous campaign, scored first. Then we ran riot. That was a strong Rangers team with the likes of Terry Butcher, Ian Durrant, Richard Gough, Ally McCoist, Gary Stevens, Mark Walters, Ray Wilkins and Chris Woods in it.

The stand-out moment for me, and for many other Rangers fans, that afternoon was the Wilkins goal. It is seared into my memory banks to this day. Stevens took a throw-in out on the right, the ball got headed out to the edge of the Celtic penalty box from where Wilkins unleashed an unstoppable volley into the net. It was stunning.

Rangers had just installed television screens in all of the concourse areas at Ibrox. At half-time I went down to get a pie and a Bovril and they were showing replays of the Wilkins goal over and over again. I can remember thinking to myself: "I wonder if they're showing the same footage on the televisions to the Celtic fans in the Broomloan Road Stand just now?"

I had some scary moments at Old Firm matches over the years as well. One of the worst was when I was returning home from a cup game at Hampden one night on the Linwood supporters' bus. We were driving along Aikenhead Road and the bus was attacked. Some Celtic supporters ran out of a close as we were stuck at traffic lights and bricks came in the window.

That very same night, a Rangers supporters' bus was driving past the Celtic Supporters' Club on the London Road and a brick was thrown at it. It went through a window and hit a passenger. Tragically, he died as a result of his injuries. When I found out about what had happened later it was chilling. After all, exactly the same thing had happened on the bus I was on. It was a bit of a wake-up call. I thought: "What is this rivalry all about exactly? It's just a game of football!"

I admit I have sung my fair share of sectarian songs in my time. Not at home games. That kind of behaviour and language wouldn't have been tolerated in the area of the main stand at Ibrox where

I was billeted on match days along with my family. But at away games I belted out just about everything and anything. This was long before such conduct was outlawed in Scotland. To be honest, though, I had no idea what I was on about half the time. I just sang what the boy next to me was singing.

My father's side of the family were all Protestants and Rangers fans. But that wasn't the case on my mother's side of the family. She was one of five sisters and a couple of my aunts had married Catholic men. So I had cousins who I spent time with growing up who wore crucifixes, went to schools which started in St and were all massive Celtic supporters.

When the motor factory in Linwood was closed down in 1981 my father gave a few people he knew, neighbours and friends, jobs at the chain of shoe repair shops he ran. I can remember him telling my grandfather about somebody who was coming to work at the firm.

My grandfather said to him: "But he's a Catholic!"

My father replied: "I'm well aware of that."

My grandfather exclaimed: "But we're a Protestant firm!"

He didn't say it with any hatred. A person's religion wasn't an issue to him. It was just a generational thing. When my grandfather had been a boy, Glasgow was full of Catholic businesses and shops and Protestant businesses and shops. It was just the way it was at that time. But I can remember thinking: "That is downright weird!"

I can recall a surreal incident that sums up the utter absurdity of the rivalry between the Old Firm clubs. It took place before the Scottish Cup final with Celtic in 1989. As I walked up to the game with the Rangers supporters who had been on my bus from Linwood we gave the full repertoire of songs, The Billy Boys, The Sash and so on, lusty renditions.

Next to the turnstile we were queuing at to get in to the stadium there was a row of police and then a line of Celtic fans waiting to file through their turnstile. Obviously, we gave them an absolute earful.

As I was screaming abuse, I caught the eye of a boy on the other side of the thin blue line who I recognised. I was in a football team in Port Glasgow with him. I had played alongside him that very morning. He was giving as good as he got.

I thought: "Haud on a second here! I was playing football with you earlier! Now you're a dirty Fenian bastard and I'm a dirty Orange bastard?" We both stopped what we were doing and cracked up laughing.

That day just got more ridiculous when the game kicked off. The Celtic captain Roy Aitken conned the referee Bob Valentine and took a throw in that should never have been awarded to his side. Joe Miller went up the park and scored what turned up the only goal of the game. I was standing about as close to that controversial incident as was possible. I missed the goal because I was too busy screaming abuse at the linesman. But that was a rare failure at that time.

FOR Rangers supporters of my generation, winning the Premier League title at the end of the 1986/87 season was an emotional experience. I had spent a long, long time watching my team struggle and fail before that.

In the 1979/80 campaign, the first season I had gone along to see matches at Ibrox regularly, we finished fifth in the top flight and failed to qualify for Europe. Things didn't get much better for many years.

The stadium was rebuilt between 1978 and 1981 and there were limited resources for the manager, John Greig, to spend on players. There was an occasional success. But mostly there was bitter disappointment. The football was often absolute dross. Looking back now, I was definitely scarred by it all growing up.

The highlight of Souness's time in charge of Rangers for me, along with many, many other fans, was undoubtedly that first Scottish title win. I wasn't one of the 10,000 supporters who travelled to the penultimate league game against Aberdeen up at Pittodrie. I wasn't there to see Butcher head a Cooper cross into the net in the second half into to secure a 1-1 draw which gave us the single point we needed to clinch the trophy. I listened to events unfold on radio.

But I was certainly in my seat in the main stand at Ibrox the following weekend for the match with St. Mirren when we were presented with the trophy. I must admit, I was pretty choked up about it all. It was the first time I had lived through Rangers winning the league. We had won the domestic Treble in both 1976 and 1978 when Jock Wallace was manager. But I was just a laddie at that time.

After the St. Mirren game, I was one of the very last people to leave the stadium. The team had been presented with the trophy and had carried out the customary lap of honour around the pitch. The players had all headed in to the changing room to continue their celebrations and the fans had all dispersed singing and dancing into the night.

But I stayed behind. At the time, my dad always left games a bit early so he could head into the city to lock up his shops. I would wait for him at the ground and get collected as he headed back to Bridge of Weir where we were living by then.

My seat was in the main stand just to the right of the directors' box and as I waited I looked over. Standing there by himself staring out onto the deserted pitch was David Holmes.

Lawrence Marlborough, the Nevada-based businessman, had installed Holmes, who at that time was the chief executive of the house building firm John Lawrence UK, on the board to represent his interests when he had bought the majority of the shareholding two years earlier.

Holmes was the one who had recognised the enormous untapped commercial potential of the club and who had set about increasing revenue through official club merchandise and corporate hospitality. He also made changes to the wage structure.

I was just a boy of 14 at the time. But I shuffled along the seats to the wooden divide.

I called out: "Mr Holmes?"

He replied: "Yes, what is it son?"

I asked him: "Have you got a minute?"

He came over to where I was standing. I took my scarf off and wrapped it around his neck.

I explained: "The players and coaches all got scarves thrown onto the pitch to wear. But I think you've done just as much to win us the league as they have. You brought Graeme Souness to Rangers. Thank you."

Many years later, when I was living and working down in London, an acquaintance of mine found himself doing some business with David Holmes. I told him that story and he relayed it the next time they met.

Apparently, Holmes responded: "I remember that well! In fact, I remember that like it was yesterday. I tell people the story about that young boy that day myself."

It was the first time I had met and spoken to a Rangers director. It wouldn't be the last.

CHAPTER 2
PLAYING FOR THE ENEMY

"I could help you become a professional footballer Craig. But there are maybe things you would need to do for me."

Jim Torbett, Celtic youth coach.

I LEFT school as soon as I possibly could. My older sister Fiona is an accountant to trade now. She was bright, driven, studied hard, got good qualifications and went on to university. Personally, I just saw it all as a bit of an inconvenience. I was always desperate to get out. Everything my parents said to me about applying myself properly and doing well fell on deaf ears..

Every now and again I would make an effort to get into things. I always struggled with English. But I can remember on one occasion being given an essay to write about emotions, feelings and senses. I sat at my desk and thought: "You know what? I'm going to give this education caper a go!"

I wrote about attending a Rangers game at Ibrox. I wrote about the build-up, about the nervous sensation in my stomach as I walked up Paisley Road West before kick-off, about all of the different sights and sounds and smells of match day. I was dead chuffed with it when I was finished. I was certain I was going to get an A.

But a couple of days later I got it flung back in my face. The teacher yelled: "Rangers! Seriously? Rangers! Is that all you can write about?" That was the end of my interest in English.

When I turned 16 in 1989 I was out of there. My first job was as an administration assistant with the Scottish Office at St. Andrews House on West Nile Street. I put letters in envelopes, punched holes in sheets of paper and filed away folders. I lasted ten months doing that. Then I ran out of the place screaming.

I was working there when Rangers signed Mo Johnston. A lady called Margaret McGonigle sat next to me. Margaret was Celtic daft. She was the one who broke the news which rocked Scottish football to me. She used a few choice expletives as she did so I seem to recall!

A lot of Rangers fans were just as upset about it. Johnston was the first high-profile Catholic player we had signed in our history. Personally, I saw it more as two fingers being stuck up to Celtic. Our fierce city rivals had paraded the striker as a signing just weeks before and hailed him as the returning Messiah. I saw far more positives in the fact that we had got him than negatives.

Signing a Catholic player was something that Rangers were always going to do. Graeme Souness was married to a Catholic and made it clear when he was appointed manager that he wouldn't adhere to our traditional signing policy. I don't think they could have topped the way they did it in the end. It was an outrageous piece of brinksmanship.

The people who were protesting about it were brought up in a different era. I don't think they hated Catholics as such. I just think they felt that is the way it had always been and the way it should remain. I had no cause to complain anyway. As a boy I had played for Celtic for two seasons myself.

I was football-daft when I was young. I started off turning out for a team called Linwood Rangers. A lad called Paul Lambert was two years above me in that side. Even then, you could see he was a fantastic talent. It was no great surprise when he went on to turn professional and star for St. Mirren, Motherwell, Borussia Dortmund, where he won the Champions League, Celtic and Scotland.

Like every boy in the west of Scotland, I wanted to be a professional footballer too. I suppose I was fairly promising. Certainly, I got a fair few phone calls from clubs asking me to go and play for them. St. Mirren Boys Club, Renfrew Waverley, Pollok and others all got in touch.

One day I came in and my father said: "Celtic Boys Club have been on the phone. They want you to go and play for them." So that was what I did. The reason was pretty simple. Out of all of the teams which wanted to sign for me they were by far the best. But my dad did raise an eyebrow at the time. He asked me: "Do you really want to go to Celtic son?"

But the fact I was a Rangers fan didn't really cross my mind. One thing made my decision up for me. The league sponsor at the time used to produce a preview publication before every season. Inside it were profiles of all the clubs and their squads. They contained all the usual information for the players, date of birth, height, position and so on. The last category listed was previous club.

Around a quarter of the players had been through Celtic Boys Club. Aberdeen, Dundee United, Hearts - every club apart from Rangers basically - had at least one player, and normally around three or four players, who had turned out for them. As a young boy who wanted to be a professional footballer I thought: "That is the place to go!"

Celtic Boys Club was well known as a good breeding ground for professional footballers. Despite being Rangers fans, I think my pals were quite proud of the fact I was going to play for such a prominent club. There was some inevitable banter of course. But it was all good-natured and jovial. It isn't all that uncommon for Celtic fans to play for Rangers as kids and for Rangers fans to play for Celtic as kids.

I was always a centre half or a central midfield player. But when I got to Celtic they started playing me at centre forward. I was never a striker. I can recollect playing up front in a cup semi-final against Rangers at Benburb Park. I was up front. The game finished up a draw and we lost on penalties. Brian O'Neill, who went on to do the best out of all of us and played for Celtic, Aberdeen, Wolfsburg, Derby County, Preston North End and Scotland, missed a spot kick and we got knocked out. It was the only time Rangers ever beat Celtic while I was there.

During the game, a ball got played over the top of the Rangers centre half. I wasn't the fastest. But I ran in at an angle and caught the goalkeeper off guard as he was coming off his line. I thought: "Right, I either knock it over his head or I take it round him. Either way I've scored." It was 0-0 late in the game. I was positive I was about to win the match and send us through to the final.

But just as the ball came over my shoulder I caught sight of the Rangers crest on the keeper's jersey out of the corner of my eye. In a split second I thought:"Fuck me! I'm just about to score the winner for Celtic against Rangers!" I blew it. It should have been a tap-in winner. Instead the ball hit me on the back of the head. It was definitely caused by the realisation of what I was about to do.

I remember one other thing about that day. The parents of the Rangers players had all parked near to the door that we came out of a long time after the final whistle. When you lost with Celtic Boys Club you tended to spend quite a while in the changing room being spoken to about it by the coaches afterwards. It was considered unacceptable.

When we did finally emerge the mothers and fathers of the opposing team were all sitting in their cars, with the windows open, listening to Orange tunes. Then they started giving us abuse.

Despite being a Rangers supporter, I was getting it as well because, to them, I was a Celtic player. It was an eye opener for me. I was embarrassed fans of my club were acting that way. It made me once again question the enmity between the two city rivals. To see grown adults acting in that way towards children was pathetic. I was very uncomfortable with it. It was another defining moment in my attitude towards the Old Firm divide.

There was another more humorous moment when I was at Celtic. In a Scottish Cup game against Renfrew Waverley I was up against a centre half who I knew from Linwood who went to St. Brendan's High School.

There were a couple of undesirables sitting at the side of the park drinking a bottle of fortified wine. They were supporting a team they presumably thought was Rangers - because of their blue strip - against Celtic.

We were defending a corner and I – a Rangers-supporting Protestant - was standing at the halfway line next to their centre half - who was a Celtic-supporting Catholic. One of the drunks shouted over to my opponent.

"Big yin!" he screamed. "Just boot him up the arse! If the big Fenian bastard says anything about it I'll come on and do him!"

We looked at each other and burst out laughing. If only they knew the truth!

Frank Cairney ran Celtic Boys Club back then. He was a stern individual and had a definite presence about him. When he walked past you stood up straight. There was a famous story about him, which may well have been apocryphal, but it certainly put the fear of death into me. In one of the changing rooms at the Barrowfield training ground there was a big chunk out of the concrete wall.

The story went that two boys had been chatting as Frank was dissecting the game after the final whistle. He looked over and then launched a glass bottle at them. It missed and took a chunk out of the wall. The message went out that the hole wasn't to be repaired. It was a warning to boys that when Frank spoke you listened. He never coached me. He used to take the older teams. But he still had an aura about him and was not to be crossed.

Barrowfield had two changing rooms. They were connected by the shower block. One night the older boys were in the left-hand changing room and we were in the right-hand changing room. Our keeper at the time was a hilarious character who used to do fantastic impersonations. That night he was standing with his back to the showers doing an impression of Frank Cairney.

"Yous are all shite!" he bellowed. "Yous are all a fucking disgrace! Yous don't even deserve to play for the Celtic!"

We were all doubled up laughing, tears streaming down our faces. Then Frank appeared through the showers. The goalie didn't realise he was there and he carried on with his routine. When he finally clocked him, his face turned a different colour and he legged it.

The goalie went on to become a sports journalist and a football pundit on TV and radio. Years later I was at a fund-raising event for the Second Chance charity the former Rangers player Alex Rae runs and he was there. Sons of Struth was up and running by this time. I went over and said hello.

I asked him: "I take it you know I'm the Sons of Struth guy?"

He said: "Aye, of course."

"But do you remember how you know me?"

"I do."

"Well, I owe you a big thank you then. I'm getting attacked from all sides. If that came out it would have been another thing for people to hit me with. You haven't told anybody at all have you?"

"It's nobody's business Craig."

But I was grateful.

A man called Jim Torbett also coached a team at Celtic Boys Club and at the start of my second season there I found myself in it. He was a different character to Frank Cairney. He still had a presence about him. But he didn't strike fear into you in quite the same way. He was actually an easier man to talk to. It later transpired, though, there were sinister reasons for the kindness he showed us.

There were comments made and things which happened which, at the time, went over my head because of the age I was. In fact, it was only many years later when he was charged with sexually abusing boys at the club and imprisoned that it actually dawned on me what had gone on. It was a horrible moment. It sent a shiver down my spine.

My head started spinning as I thought back to situations which arose during my time at the club. I wasn't personally affected directly. Nor did I see any abuse take place. But things which were said to me, phrases which were used and scenarios which occurred came flooding back to me.

I can vividly remember one occasion when Jim Torbett was running a group of us home after a game. I was getting dropped off in the city centre and ended up in the front of the big Mercedes that he drove.

He asked me: "Would your father be proud if you became a professional football player Craig."

I answered: "Aye, of course he would."

He replied: "That's good. I could help you become a professional footballer Craig. But there are maybe things you would need to do for me."

At the time, the remark meant nothing at all to me. I just presumed he wanted me to wash his car or polish the boots or something. I was just a teenager. Child abuse wasn't something I was aware of. But as soon as the allegations against him emerged that specific conversation immediately came back to me. It stopped me in my tracks. I am sure that was how the abuse started.

Jim Torbett had been drummed out of Celtic years before. I was unaware of this when I was there. It only became public knowledge during the court case. That, as much as anything, troubled me. If somebody had done the right thing at the time then boys in the future wouldn't have suffered the fate they did. It saddens and sickens me to this day to know that people within the club knew of incidents and insinuations years before and did and said nothing.

It was a different era. I am a youth coach now and there are a lot of safeguards for children. Every club has to have child protection officers for example. But just because those sort of guidelines weren't in place years ago doesn't forgive anybody who allowed child abuse to happen at Celtic Boys Club.

I left Celtic Boys Club after two years. With hindsight, I shouldn't have joined them. It was a mistake. I didn't improve as a player and it actually put me off football for a while. It took a long time for me to get my appetite back for the game I had grown up loving. When I finally did, Jim Torbett was charged and ultimately jailed. The revelations which emerged during the court case sickened me.

I went and played for Port Glasgow Rangers for a season. Then I chucked it. I had chances in the game and I burned them all. I managed to blag a job as a salesman at a local garage. I must have been alright at it as I ended up doing it for over 20 years.

I spent a spell as the director of an industrial cleaning company down in London during that time. Some years later I started my own small business supplying the same services in Glasgow and did that quite happily until I became involved in the campaign for change at Rangers.

I got married, bought a house in Cambuslang, had kids. When my son Ben started to play football he joined a local team called Stranraer Boys Club. I went along as a parent to watch him and became friendly with a guy called Brian Miller who was coaching him. We ended up becoming good pals and going to Rangers games together. He helped to run the Drumsagard Loyal. We went to matches home and away, went to Europe together, enjoyed some fun times.

I can remember going to the Champions League game against Unirea in Romania in 2009 with Brian. It rained the entire time we were there. We drew the game and there was trouble in the stands. We had gas canisters fired into us and all sorts. But the stewards were terrible.

An Irish tricolour flag got thrown at us about at half-time. The stewards came in heavy handed. I thought: "The Unirea fans have obviously thrown that in as a wind up. But they're miles away. How did they get that in here?" It turned out it was actually the stewards themselves who had lobbed it in.

Brian soon drafted me in to help look after the team below my son's age group. That is when I first got involved in coaching. I didn't want to go into it half-cocked. So I got in touch with a guy I knew who ran the Jimmy Johnstone Club at Toryglen.

Jim Simonetti was a very well-known and respected coach in youth circles in Glasgow. I asked him if I could go and help out. I just wanted to watch him do some drills and routines. But when I arrived he had arranged for my to do the first part of my coaching badges. He was getting the SFA to put all of his coaches through their badges. As a result, I had done my badges before I had even coached.

It was when I was coaching at Drumsagard - which was what Stranraer Boys Club became known as - that I met Sandy Chugg. We started coaching around the same time, found out we were both Rangers fans and our friendship started from there.

We ended up coaching a team together for a while. But it was pretty disastrous. We were like the Laurel and Hardy of youth football. He would talk to me and I would be focused on the game. He would tell me so-and-so would be better player here or there. I would just ignore him or tell him to shut up. We had great respect for each other's coaching and knowledge. But when you are standing at the side of the park then there is only going to be one gaffer and we both wanted to be the boss. We only lasted for four games together. But we stayed the best of pals.

I had heard the name Sandy Chugg somewhere before. But I couldn't remember where. It nagged away at me for a while. It was only after we had been friends for two or three months that the penny finally dropped. One day it just came to me.

I remembered him from when I was in my teens and had started going to Rangers games home and away. Hooliganism was a major problem in football in the 1980s. You would hear stories about fights between rival groups of casuals. The name Sandy Chugg would often come up in conversation. He was a notorious ringleader who ran with this crazy team called the Inter City Firm

He hit the news at the World Cup in 1998. The Scottish casuals went to Salou in Spain for a fortnight so they could sneak into France undetected by the authorities. I think they had a ruck organised with like-minded individuals of other nationalities in Marseille.

But their scheme was rumbled and their double decker bus got stopped at the border. I could still remember a photo in the papers. Sandy was leaning against the windscreen on the top deck with some of his associates. The headline in the Daily Record was "Scotland's Shame!".

It came up in conversation one night. It finally clicked and I said: "No way! Not our Sandy!" I grilled him about it and he started to tell me all the stories about his escapades.

He had spent some time in jail for dealing drugs. But when I met him he was a completely reformed character. He had three children and lived in a nice new housing estate in Cambuslang. We had boys of a similar age.

Before I left the area, Brian, Sandy and myself would all used to go Rangers games on the Drumsagard Loyal supporters bus with our sons Kyle, Elliott, Nathan and Ben for a year or two. Our boys picked up the enthusiasm and the passion for the Ibrox club which their fathers had. I can remember thinking: "I was like that once!" They were good times to be a supporter.

CHAPTER 3

LONDON GEORGE

"I'm not George. George hasn't turned up."

London George, Rangers fan.

I DON'T think any Rangers fan ever really believed, not deep down, that what happened to our beloved Ibrox club in 2012 was actually possible. For its supporters, Rangers is an institution. It is, in many ways, like a church to us. We felt it would always be there no matter what misfortune befell us and what financial hardships we faced.

Craig Whyte, the Motherwell-born venture capitalist we had all hailed as a saviour and applauded down Edmiston Drive after he had bought Rangers for £1 from Sir David Murray the year before, put the club into administration in February that year. It soon emerged Her Majesty's Revenue and Customs was chasing £9 million in unpaid PAYE and VAT.

It also came to light that Whyte, who many Gers supporters had continued to back after a BBC Scotland documentary revealed he had previously been banned as a director for seven years, had paid for the purchase with £25 million he had received from finance firm Ticketus for advance season ticket sales.

Charles Green, the former chief executive of Sheffield United, appeared from nowhere fronting a consortium of businessmen. He was given preferred bidder status by the administrators Duff and Phelps. But his group's proposed offer of nine pence in the pound to creditors was rejected by HMRC in June and the club's parent company was placed into liquidation.

I think a big problem at that time was that we desperately wanted to believe what first Whyte and then Green were telling us. If somebody speaks confidently, positively and optimistically about your club then fans are, especially after some difficult times, quite happy to accept it because you are desperate for it to be true.

So when a bold and brash character like Green came in and took over and started making all sorts of grandiose claims about what he was going to do and where he was going to take the club people bought it for the simple reason they wanted to believe him. But it was nothing new. It had been the case for years.

It went back to Sir David Murray's time in charge. When Murray appeared on the scene at first it was wonderful. He was a young and ambitious businessman with an abundance of money who was prepared to invest heavily in the club and propel us to new heights on and off the field. After years of failure and mediocrity, we bought into that.

As time wore on, though, the spending grew less and less lavish and the quality on the field gradually deteriorated. He became held in lower and lower regard by many fans. When stories began to emerge about the club being investigated for a tax avoidance scheme called an Employee Benefit Trust which had been used to pay players we chose to ignore them. As a support, we were probably caught off guard. We would hold onto the good stories and hope they were true and dismiss the bad ones.

In the end, Murray sold a football club which had a potential tax bill of tens of millions of pounds hanging over it as a consequence of the use of EBTs for £1 to a suspect figure. But it was Lloyds Banking Group which actually sold Rangers. They were, after insisting on having their employee Donald Muir appointed to the board, effectively running the club by that stage. They got the £18 million they were owed. They were happy.

When Whyte took over there was both negative and positive publicity surrounding him. I wasn't alone in wanting to believe the good stuff. He was famously described as having "wealth off the radar" by Keith Jackson of the Daily Record when he emerged on the scene. That sounded pretty good to me and many others.

But I can remember looking at how the man dressed in his first days at the club and thinking: "Sorry, this just doesn't add up! If I had the money he was supposed to have I wouldn't be wearing plastic shoes! I would have a pair of Gucci's!" He always looked uncomfortable and unconvincing in his appearances on television.

As time wore on, it became increasingly obvious he wasn't all he was cracked up to be. Unfortunately, the truth can sometimes be what the majority of people want it to be. As I say, we wanted to believe the good and didn't want to believe the bad.

There was a lot of uncertainty about the future of Rangers in the opening weeks of 2012. But it was probably only a few days before the club was actually placed into administration, and Whyte made his now infamous night time address to a mob of angry supporters at the front door of Ibrox, that I myself decided to take action.

I phoned my friend Sandy Chugg. I said: "Look, I'm concerned. Something's going on. We don't know what it is. But surely we at least need to go and ask the question."

I asked Sandy if he would be able to get a mob of his former football hooligan friends together. My plan was to get mini-buses and vans filled up with fans and stepladders, head down to Ibrox, scale the famous blue iron gates and then handcuff ourselves to the dugouts. After that, my idea was to phone the newspapers and tell them we wouldn't move until we got an answer from somebody at Rangers about what was in the offing.

As I have mentioned, Sandy had been pretty mental in his younger years. But his response was: "Yer aff yer heid Craig!" It was like getting told by an alcoholic you have a drink problem. The proposed stunt went no further.

A few days later the club was put into administration. Sandy and I spoke about it afterwards. If we had done something that day, anything at all, it wouldn't have changed what happened. But we certainly wouldn't have had the gnawing sense of guilt that we later felt about sitting idly by and allowing it to happen.

The warning signs were all there for us. John Greig, our legendary former captain, resigned from his position on the Rangers board, ending an association with the Ibrox club which stretched back over 50 years, amid claims he had been frozen out. A television documentary revealed the owner's highly dubious background. The club was delisted from the stock exchange after failing to submit audited accounts on time.

We should have been far more tuned in to what was happening as a support. But, once again, we just didn't want to believe it. We refused to accept the bad in the stories which were emerging and we attacked those who were telling us something untoward was afoot. As fans, we did absolutely nothing. Sandy and I were angry at ourselves as a result.

When Green turned up, took over and started shouting his mouth off we quickly slipped back into our old lazy ways of thinking. Looking back, our attitude was: "Well, we've been through the bad times. Things can't possibly get any worse'. We should have seen it coming once more. But pretty quickly it became obvious all was not well in the running of the club.

When Sandy and I started to hear the bad stories - about what Whyte had done, about Green being another shadowy character with less than scrupulous methods, about how he had ripped Sheffield United apart just to make a fast buck - we decided we couldn't twiddle our thumbs any longer.

I started to analyse the Yorkshireman's public appearances. I had been a sales manager and a sales trainer previously in my career. From a professional perspective, I thought the guy was a cracking salesman. The controversial statements he came out with and the madcap stunts he pulled ingratiated him to a support hurting badly from how their club had been treated. For example, he gave out free cups of coffee and tea to supporters queuing outside Ibrox to buy season books. It is pretty simple. But it is highly effective.

But before the end of his first season at the club Green had, despite claiming to have contracted "Rangersitis" and vowing to stay until the Champions League music Zadoc the Priest was blaring out at Ibrox again, resigned as chief executive.

That followed alarming claims about the takeover which Green had led the previous summer by Whyte and his admission he had "shafted" the previous owner. An internal investigation was launched by Deloitte and Pinsent Masons, at considerable expense to the club, to determine if there was any truth in the allegations. It was later shown there was no foundation to them. However, to date, nobody has seen the reports.

Green had also described his business partner Imran Ahmad, who had been appointed as club commercial director, as "my Paki friend" in an interview with a newspaper. He had been charged with using racist and offensive language by the SFA as a result.

The accounts published in October showed he walked away with nearly £1 million after spending less than a year at Rangers. He was paid a £333,077 annual salary, received a £360,000 bonus for the club beating part-time opponents to the Third Division, pocketed benefits which amounted to £22,449 and a collected severance payment of £217,850.

Green returned briefly as a "consultant" the following season. But he only lasted a few weeks before a furious reaction by supporters resulted in him being removed from his £1,000-a-month position. One of his last acts was to have serious repercussions for the club long after he had disappeared from the scene. He sold the vast majority of his shares to Sandy Easdale.

Speculation about the brothers James and Sandy Easdale, who had served time for VAT fraud, buying into the club had first emerged the previous year. The Daily Record pictured the Greenock businessmen, who were owners of, among other firms, McGill's Buses, on its front page being given a tour of Ibrox. Given all we had just been through, having somebody with a criminal past was the last thing supporters needed or wanted.

A MEETING at Ibrox in the August of 2013 was a turning point for me personally. Craig Mather, a shareholder who had taken over from Green as chief executive, Brian Stockbridge, the financial director, Ian Hart, a non-executive director, and Ally McCoist, the manager, made themselves available to answer questions and attempt to alleviate the growing concerns of supporters about what was happening behind the scenes.

Representatives of the Rangers Supporters Assembly, Association and Trust, the three main fans groups, were all invited. And "selected season ticket holders" were also asked along . In total, there were around 200 people at the gathering. Together, they were allowed to ask 50 questions.

I was driving in my car near the stadium at the time listening to a radio report on it. The phrase "selected season ticket holders" really stuck in my throat. I said to myself: "I'm not a member of the assembly, the association or the trust. But I've been a season ticket holder for 30 years. Why can't I go?" It really irked me.

Chris Graham, a prominent internet blogger and Tweeter, was interviewed by BBC Radio Scotland coming out of the meeting. I had seen him on television a couple of times previously during the dark days of administration and I can remember being very impressed. He was well spoken and clearly knew what he was talking about.

In the radio interview he expressed his disappointment that board members had waffled their way through answers and jumped onto the next question without giving full and satisfactory explanations. I was absolutely incensed by what I was hearing.

I thought: "I would've loved to have asked questions at that meeting. If they'd tried to move on without answering properly they would've had a hard job. No way would I have let them do that." I was disappointed the people in that meeting not only didn't represent me but also didn't act like I would have.

I sat in rooms and spoke with multi-millionaires during our subsequent campaign. But I didn't take any smash from anybody. That frustrating experience, coupled with the guilt Sandy and I felt at not doing anything as the club was plunged into administration, probably led to the formation of Sons of Struth.

I started going online to try and learn more about what was happening at the club. I wasn't a huge fan of the Rangers cyber community. I had dabbled with it. But what I discovered very early on when it came to the various chat rooms and internet forums was if you weren't in agreement with the party line then you were branded a Celtic supporter. Anybody with an alternative opinion was quickly chased. To my mind, they weren't good places for healthy debate. They were good for ridiculing people with different views to yourself.

In the years before Sons of Struth was formed, I had probably been on Rangers sites around half a dozen times. If a major signing was in the offing I would maybe log on to see if anybody had any insight into what was happening. Generally speaking, though, I didn't enjoy the experience and stayed well clear.

However, after the club went into administration I felt compelled to see what was happening. I was working at a desktop computer in an office selling life insurance at that particular time. Logging onto football websites wasn't advisable. So I found a mobile site I could sneak a look at on my phone called Rangers Rumours.

I would check the newspapers when I went into my work to see what the latest was. Then I would go online to try and find out what the back story was. I was never a great poster on it. I just used it to gain information.

A Rangers supporter who posted on that site pretty regularly would always sign off as "George". He was a Scot who was based down in London. He was very interested in Craig Whyte and what his intentions had been. He was clearly deeply concerned for his club. He was convinced money was still going sideways.

George put up a post one day which revealed he had just paid to have a leaflet printed which outlined his beliefs about the Whyte era, his suspicions about Green and his fears about the new regime. He then stated he was coming up to Glasgow to hand it out at the front door of the stadium at ten o'clock one Friday morning. He said he would be willing to speak to any of his fellow supporters who turned up. Like so many of us by that stage, he had just had enough.

I talked to Sandy about it. I told him: "I'm going to go along to this and hear the guy out. I'll give him a few minutes of my time and listen to what he has to say. He might be the biggest liar in the world. But I'm going to go along and see all the same. There's no harm in hearing him out."

When I got to Ibrox at the allotted time there was a group of a dozen or so Rangers fans gathered around one man outside the school across from the main stand. I parked the car and wandered over to where they were. The first thing the bloke said was: "I'm not George. George hasn't turned up. There aren't any leaflets."

The assembled supporters were clearly quite disappointed. But I clicked straight away that it actually was George. He started giving everyone his views about what had happened under Whyte. I asked him: "I've always wondered what the point of Whyte getting involved was. How did he benefit from doing so?" He outlined what he believed had happened. His theories were staggering.

The meeting lasted for 20 minutes or so and then people started to disperse. The guy said to me: "Have you got a minute? You seem to have picked up very quickly on what I'm saying." I said: "Well, I don't think it's difficult. I get it."

We wandered off to his car and had a blether. He eventually admitted he was George and revealed he had been worried somebody at the club would try to infiltrate the gathering to see what was being discussed. He said he was still concerned about the current regime and that interested me. He had meetings in the city planned for that weekend. But we agreed to speak again on the Monday at my parents' flat just along the road in Kinning Park.

Sandy Chugg came along on that occasion. London George turned up wearing a pair of blue patent leather cowboy boots. He was a wee chap who was in his late forties or early fifties. He cut a bit of a bizarre figure if I am being honest. But he came in, sat down and three concerned Rangers fans spoke to each other for two hours about their fears for their club.

We had a league game the following night against Berwick at Ibrox. London George promised to give us the leaflets he had talked about. They basically outlined his theories about Whyte. Sandy and I agreed to distribute them at the match. We had no name as such at that time.

London George was never in Sons of Struth. But he probably provided the spark which got us started. We will be eternally grateful to him for that. I am still in contact with him sporadically on social media and by text message. As I got to know him after that, I grew to believe he was an accountant to trade. I would describe him as being educated in life.

His name wasn't actually George. Last I heard of him, he was someone the police were interested in talking to.

Basically, though, London George was just a Bear who was worried about his club. He spurred us on to do something. He put leaflets in our hands. That was significant. We soon became well known for that. If it hadn't been for him we may never have come up with the idea. It was a key development in how we evolved as a group.

There was no name on the first three batches of leaflets which we handed out. People just took them. But pretty soon folk were coming up to us at games and saying: "Is that your new leaflet?" They were turning up expecting and looking for printed information from us.

I think the fact that we weren't started on social media was important. The people who go online think everybody is online. But they aren't. Far from it in fact. Only a small percentage of supporters are. Getting our message out to all of the fans who were turning up at Ibrox probably helped with the numbers who got involved in our protests.

After we had launched officially as Sons of Struth – through the simple act of setting up a Facebook page - I often asked myself: "How did this go from a page on a social media website to tens of thousands of fans at Ibrox protesting?" I think the leaflets we handed out were significant in attracting the numbers we got behind us.

A lot of people accused me of doing Sons of Struth for an ego trip. But I never got any satisfaction out of it. Do you know what? I was actually disgusted that I had to step up and take action. It took up vast amounts of my personal time and my professional time.

I didn't want to be a figurehead. My motivation was simple. I was fed up of my football club being destroyed by rogues, scoundrels and vagabonds. My natural reaction was to stand up against it. Don't get me wrong, there were some very proud moments along the way. But the majority of the time it just sickened me that I had to do it in the first place.

I started up a Facebook page on the way out of the front door of my house before the Berwick game on August 27, 2013. Bizarrely, the name Sons of Struth just popped into my head. There is a definite pride when you read about the Bill Struths, Scot Symons and William Wiltons, all these great men who have run Rangers over the years.

It saddened me to see where the club was at that particular time. We were once run by men with principles whose priority was to do the right thing for the club. Struth was lodged in my subconscious.

Struth is the longest serving manager in the Ibrox club's history. He was in charge for a total of 34 years from 1920 to 1954. During that stretch he won a record 18 Scottish titles as well as the Scottish Cup 10 times and the League Cup twice. He masterminded our first double in 1928 and oversaw our first treble in 1949. He remains, with no fewer than 30 trophies to his name, one of the most decorated managers in British football history.

But he did more for Rangers than bring silverware and sporting success to the club. The former stonemason and professional athlete from Edinburgh was a strict disciplinarian and was responsible for instilling many of our core values and creating many of our traditions. He insisted, for example, on his players always wearing a collar and tie and maintaining the highest standards of behaviour and dress.

There is a famous quote from Bill Struth which is known by virtually every Rangers supporter. It sums up the ethos of the Ibrox club.

It goes: "I have been lucky — lucky in those who were around me from the boardroom to the dressing-room. In time of stress, their unstinted support, unbroken devotion to our club and calmness in adversity eased the task of making Rangers FC the premier club in this country."

"To be a Ranger is to sense the sacred trust of upholding all that such a name means in this shrine of football. They must be true in their conception of what the Ibrox tradition seeks from them. No true Ranger has ever failed in the tradition set him."

"Our very success, gained you will agree by skill, will draw more people than ever to see it. And that will benefit many more clubs than Rangers. Let the others come after us. We welcome the chase. It is healthy for us. We will never hide from it. Never fear, inevitably we shall have our years of failure, and when they arrive, we must reveal tolerance and sanity."

"No matter the days of anxiety that come our way, we shall emerge stronger because of the trials to be overcome. That has been the philosophy of the Rangers since the days of the gallant pioneers."

People have asked me before if the Liverpool fans group Spirit of Shankly was my inspiration behind the name. I honestly can't remember. I suppose it must have been sitting in my memory banks somewhere. Essentially I just thought Sons of Struth could be shortened to SOS. There certainly wasn't hours of debate or much agonising put into the name. It just popped into my head as I had my laptop on my knees. It came to me in seconds.

I can remember one fan who had a Rangers Facebook page himself with a large number, several thousand, of followers contacting me soon after we started. He said: "What you're doing is great. You'll overtake the number of followers I have easily." I thought: "He has to be kidding. We'll get a couple of hundred." But he was dead right. We passed that number quite quickly.

After I came up with the name Sons of Struth, I sat down I asked myself: "What are we actually saying? What is our message? What do we want out of this? What would make Rangers fans happier? What do we stand for?" So Sandy Chugg and I put our heads together and we decided upon three aims. This is what we came up with.

1) To protect and safeguard the stadium.

We had seen what had happened with Coventry City and Leeds

United. They ended up in financial predicaments which meant they had to surrender ownership of their stadiums. We did not want Rangers to end up in that situation.

2) To get a clean set of audited accounts.

Having worked in management before, I appreciated a set of accounts didn't tell you every single detail about a company. You could quite easily hide things in accounts. Indeed, I had done it before myself when I worked in the motor trade. They are nothing more than an abbreviation of a business's activities over a certain period of time. I felt getting accounts the common fan could look at and understand where the money had gone to was important.

When the audited accounts finally came out in October there were black holes all over them. No Rangers fan could look at them and say: "Yep, I'm happy, I know where the money has gone." There were huge sums filed under ambiguous headings like "IPO costs".

3) To have a board of directors we could be proud of and trust.

At that stage, Craig Mather was the chief executive, Brian Stockbridge was the financial director, James Easdale had not long joined as a non-executive director and Ian Hart and Phil Cartmell were also involved.

Walter Smith, our legendary former manager, had resigned as chairman after just a few months on the board, a few weeks earlier. In a strongly-worded statement he hit out at a "highly-dysfunctional environment which has not been good for the club" and revealed "recent further disruption which has rendered the board less effective and efficient than it ought to have been". His parting shot was "it is clear that boardroom change is required".

The Sons of Struth Facebook page soon snowballed. I got a log-in for Follow Follow, which is the largest supporters' internet message board, and various others, including Gers Net and started posting. Most were completely supportive. A couple, though, I was unable to gain access to. It was downright bizarre. Because we were posting on Follow Follow we immediately became blocked by the likes of Rangers Media. It was a sad state of affairs.

We booked a suite in the Swallow Hotel on Paisley Road West one night. We posted on our Facebook page: "We are concerned Rangers fans who aren't happy with the current direction of the club. If you feel the same as us then come to this public meeting." I also posted on various internet forums to generate interest in the event.

It cost £150 to pay for the room and Sandy and I put in £75 each to pay for it. About 100 people turned up. There were very few people there who I knew at that time. But many of those there that night have since gone on to become close friends.

There were also some prominent Rangers fans there who have helped us financially and who we formed strong bonds with. Billy Montgomery, who is in the Rangers Fans Fighting Fund, Gordon Dinnie, the Rangers Supporters Trust chairman, and Mark Dingwall, who runs the Follow Follow website, were among them.

Sandy and I introduced ourselves at the public meeting and spoke for a few minutes about our unhappiness at the questions which had not been answered. We asked some questions of our own. What do fans want to happen at the club? What do people want to do? Do they want to do anything? What can Sons of Struth do in the future?

With the backing we received that evening, we felt we could take the next step. The feedback we received told us that if we tried something on a larger scale it would be enthusiastically supported. The seeds were sown that night for our protest at the Stenhousemuir game on Saturday, September 28. That was, if you like, the first public appearance of Sons of Struth.

After the meeting, we adjourned to the bar. It took me nearly an hour to get out of the room because so many people wanted to speak to me. When I finally got to reception and asked for the bill and got the £150 out to pay, I was told: "It's been settled." Somebody had left the meeting and paid for the room anonymously.

CHAPTER 4

WE KNOW WHERE YOU LIVE

"The board is aware that certain individuals are holding meetings and inciting fans to unruly behaviour. This has been reported to the police."

Statement on the official Rangers Football Club website.

IN the build-up to the Stenhousemuir protest, I received a phone call inviting me to a meeting which Jim McColl, the well-known businessman who is, with an estimated personal fortune of £800 million, one of Scotland's richest men, was holding with Rangers supporters groups.

You sometimes hear footballers talking about getting an international call-up for the first time. Very often they will say: "I thought it was one of my team mates at the wind-up". Well, that was what moment was like for me.

In my eyes, Sons of Struth hadn't actually done anything. I just thought: "What the hell am I getting invited for?" At that stage, we still had no idea how public our efforts were going to become. I think a lot of other people realised how big what we were doing was going to be before we did ourselves.

My compadre Sandy Chugg had also been contacted and asked to attend. But he thought it would be for the best if I went by myself. He felt I had more experience of business than he had. I'm quite sure that, at the back of his mind, he feared being linked with a former football casual wouldn't help the group's profile.

Personally, I had no issues with it myself. I thought people would be well aware of Sandy and his colourful past. He was a reformed character. But he was concerned it could impact on the efforts of the group and declined to attend.

I have been in some beautiful boardrooms in the course of my career. But the venue for that meeting at the Clyde Blowers offices in East Kilbride was right up there. Paul Murray, the former Rangers director, was present along with Jim McColl. It was all a bit surreal.

Also in attendance were prominent Rangers fans I had seen speaking on television and knew of by reputation. I felt like a bit of an imposter. I thought: "I'm in the wrong movie here." But after a few minutes, I piped up and got involved in the conversation.

The departure of Malcolm Murray as chairman that summer had caused concern among the institutional investors who had put money into Rangers at a share offering at the end of 2012. They were alarmed about the lack of corporate governance at the club without him there to represent them. They approached Jim McColl and Paul Murray and asked them to help restore order.

McColl and Murray then enlisted the assistance of Frank Blin, the former executive chairman of accountancy firm Pricewaterhouse Coopers Scotland. An extraordinary general meeting had been requisitioned at the start of that month and resolutions calling for the removal of Craig Mather, Brian Stockbridge and Bryan Smart as directors of the company and Blin and Murray to be appointed in their place had been tabled.

Blin and Murray were informed they were going to get onto the board as part of a compromise agreement with the directors they were trying to oust – only for the agreement to fall through. There was some real eye-opening information divulged at the meeting that evening.

We were told about why Frank Blin had suddenly disappeared from the scene. The nicest way to say it was that life was made decidedly uncomfortable for him. He reacted badly to that and was easily put off.

Mather had hired Jack Irvine of the public relations firm Media House, an individual who was not well liked by Rangers fans for a multitude of reasons, to represent him after his rivals' move. His new representative had wasted no time in warning Blin, McColl and Murray of what lay ahead for them with him on the case.

The former tabloid newspaper editor stated: "They have now stepped out of their comfort zones and are going to find that the everyday rules of business do not apply in the world of football and the media scrutiny they now face is like nothing they will ever have known in their professional lives."

It was alarming to read that somebody who was employed by Rangers speaking in such a threatening manner.

I was impressed with Paul Murray. The fact he had been a Rangers director was something I respected no matter what some of his critics said about him. But I immediately realised Jim McColl wasn't up for the fight like the rest of us. He was just a wealthy businessman with influence who wanted to do something good for the club.

It is important to note that at that point, around September time, Jim made it clear why he didn't want to get involved as a director or a shareholder. There was a public misconception that he was going to buy the club outright. That was never the case. He didn't even want to get involved. He just wanted a group in charge who he felt would run the club better.

He was in charge of £500 million of other people's money. He was contracted to invest that money in specific businesses where he had expertise and ensure his associates got a return. A football club wasn't his field. He couldn't invest. He had already had his involvement with the club queried by his partners. He was quite honest and open.

I felt he was unfairly blamed when things did go awry. Some people said: "He was going to buy Rangers. He's run away. He's left us in the lurch." That was never the case. Plus, while he may not have been prepared to put any money in personally if there had been boardroom change, he had extensive contacts in the financial world and would certainly have been able to find people who would have.

THE day before our first public protest in the Stenhousemuir game at Ibrox we booked The Louden Tavern, a well-known Rangers supporters' pub just next to the stadium, for a meeting and invited volunteers to come down. We needed people to help distribute leaflets and put banners up around the stadium.

In total, we had 120 banners made up and paid for by three

different sources, the Union Bears, Andy Smillie, a well-off supporter, and somebody who I will only be able to refer to in this book as Big Boris. The banners had a variety of slogans on them. They read "SONS OF STRUTH DEMAND THE TRUTH", "SPIVS OUT" and "NO MORE FACELESS INVESTORS".

We were attracting private individuals who were prepared to help us. Early on, we didn't touch anybody's money. The minute you do that you leave yourself open to all sorts of accusations. If somebody couldn't pay for something themselves at the time we would get the supplier to invoice them. That way, we didn't need any books or committees.

That stemmed from our experience of boys' football. People give up a lot of time and effort at that level of the game. But you did find that if a boy didn't get picked for a team then an aggrieved parent would start malicious rumours. A father would say: "He's taking money out of this club."

We were always accused of having people behind us. Who's funding you? Is it Paul Murray? Is it Malcolm Murray? Is it Brian Kennnedy? Is it Dave King? Is it Jim McColl? The truth is that we had many people who helped us out financially. But none of them had any interest in getting onto the board. Our campaign was to get rid of a board not to install a board.

Printers support Rangers. Graphic designers support Rangers. Web designers support Rangers. Everyone wants to do their bit. As the process evolved, even lawyers offered to help free of charge. People have put in £50 and people have put in thousands of pounds. The level of help we got was humbling. It wasn't just wealthy people either. Rank and file fans wanted to aid the cause.

In the public meeting at the Swallow Hotel we had people coming up to us trying to give us money. It was amazing. There was a real sense of togetherness at that meeting. As there was in the Louden Tavern the night before the game.

We needed to get a lot of people involved. We needed around 80 people to distribute leaflets instructing the fans to chant "sack the board" in the 18th and 72nd minutes. We also had a lot of banners to be displayed that day. We needed around 240 people to take them and hold them up. We needed manpower.

We put out feelers on social media. The purpose of the meeting was to lay down some ground rules. It was also to see how many people turned up. Over 100 did. That was encouraging. It made us think we could pull it off.

Sandy Chugg stood up and said a few words and then I stood up and spoke. Guidelines were given out. We explained that not everybody in the stadium was going to want to take part in our protest. We stressed if somebody didn't want to take a leaflet they should just hand it to the next person. We also were at pains to point out that the protests should only take place in the 18th and 72nd minutes.

The reason for that was that Armed Forces personnel were scheduled to be at the game. They were being invited onto the park at half-time. We had to be careful not to disrupt that. Rangers supporters have always had a high regard for our military. We felt that was a time to show respect. Sandy and I both said: "Nobody has to put a banner up at half-time. Nobody has to chant anything at half-time." We received a standing ovation from the fans in attendance.

But late on that night the club put out an official statement on their website. Some of it referred to things which had been posted on social media and internet forums which were nothing to do with Sons of Struth. But the last paragraph was a direct reference to us.

It read: "The board is aware that certain individuals are holding meetings and inciting fans to unruly behaviour. This has been reported to the police."

When the realisation hit me that the club I had supported all my life had put out a statement containing lies that I was encouraging "unruly behaviour" and explaining they had contacted the police I was sickened. It was utterly astonishing. It was painful, in fact. I have never been able to ascertain whether the authorities were alerted. But for them to even to suggest they had hurt.

We hadn't even staged a protest at this point. But they were attempting to counteract what we were doing.

I WAS sick with worry in the build-up to the game. I kept saying to myself: "Nobody's going to come! Nobody's going to turn up! This is going to fail!" I convinced myself that just Sandy and I would trap.

I can remember driving to the game feeling the same sense of anticipation as I did heading to an Old Firm game or a big European match. But we were playing part-time Third Division club Stenhousemuir. My pre-match butterflies had nothing to do with the opposition.

I drove around the back of the Copland Road Stand and pulled into Harrison Drive to park. My fears disappeared immediately. There were about 70 people standing there and kick-off was two hours away. I jumped out of the car and said: "Are you all here to see me?" Everyone nodded. The gratitude and relief I felt were incredible. I was genuinely stunned. At that moment, I knew it would work.

More and more fans turned up. They just kept arriving. Some wanted to distribute leaflets. Some wanted to put banners into the crowd. After a while, somebody came up to us and said: "They're talking about Sons of Struth on Radio Clyde."

It was the most confident I was at a game we held a protest at. In the card displays which came later I was always apprehensive about how many people would support it. But I walked into that game knowing it was going to be a success. It had to be with the support we had.

The information on the leaflet came from an internet source. Now, you had all sorts of individuals claiming all sorts of things, anonymously and otherwise, in cyberspace. Some, like the Twitter account called Charlotte Fakes for instance, had consistently been shown to be reliable. But you can't put your name to something if it is garbage.

When we got fed information we always checked it out. We got it verified. We spoke to somebody in the know. If the contacts we had built up who worked in The City of London didn't know about it then the chances are they would know somebody who did.

They came back and told us whether it was accurate or not. Then we decided whether to put our name to it. It was a system which clearly worked. I was never sued by anybody for publishing information that was incorrect. I was only sued for calling people names. If somebody took exception to the adjectives used to describe them I was damned sure the information I had was true. We found out later the leaflets even made it into the directors' box. It was an amazing day I will never forget.

Somebody at the public meeting suggested we hold up the banners and chant "sack the board" in the 18th and 72nd minutes of the game due, of course, to Rangers being founded in 1872. So that was what we did.

Sandy and I actually devised very few of the stunts which we ended up pulling. For anything inside the stadium - banners or chants – we usually turned to the Blue Order and the Union Bears. They were responsible for generating the atmosphere and spectacle at games and had been doing it for years so it made sense. They helped us greatly. They also supplied a lot of the volunteers on the ground. One of the organisers of The Blue Order - they don't court or like publicity so I won't name him – in particular had a lot of input into our activities.

My seat was near to the directors' box that day. I had a one man banner. I thought I would be the only person in my section of the main stand with one. But there were two or three there. To a man, they were standing up and joining in with the chants. I can remember one chap just in front of the media gantry with a flag. I thought: "I wonder who he is?"

My adrenalin levels were through the roof. If I could have bottled and sold the feelings I had that day I would be a multi-millionaire today. I can remember looking over at the directors' box. They were stunned. They obviously knew it was coming. But I think the ferocity and sheer size of the protests took them aback.

I decided to take my banner over and hold it above the directors' box as they walked out. Just before half-time, I went down into the concourse, sneaked along a section and came up right at the back of it.

At the meeting we had held the night before we stressed to people the need to behave responsibly. I had said: "We're using the name Struth so behave with dignity and respect people who perhaps don't want to join in."

I started looking for a seat so I didn't disrupt anybody's enjoyment of the game. I said to the guy next to me: "See this protest? I'm the guy organising it. I'm going to hold this banner up at half-time. Is that okay?" He said: "You must be Sandy's pal Craig! Crack on! My name's Mint!"

Sandy Chugg was sitting with Big Boris in the Bar '72 seats. I texted him and told them to look behind the directors' box. When they did all they could see was a banner reading: "SONS OF STRUTH DEMAND THE TRUTH".

Every single director - all of these men who, in my opinion and that of many others, were running the club badly - had to walk underneath that banner as they left. To a man, they all avoided eye contact with me. They pretended not to notice me standing there. That split second made all of the planning worth it.

I thought: "If we achieve nothing else at least you know that we don't like you. I don't know what the end game will be. But you get it. You'll never think we are naive or stupid again. You know we won't let you get away with the lies you're telling us?"

The director I took the most pleasure seeing that day was the finance director Brian Stockbridge. He looked like a rabbit in the headlights. That may sound a bit sick. But he was responsible for a lot of the wrongdoing at the club. He was employed when many "onerous contracts", as they were later described, were signed.

We have had a lot of highs during this process and that was one of them. Sandy and I met up after the game and just looked at each other in disbelief. He said: "What've we done?" In the space of two months we had gone from a Facebook page and a bunch of leaflets to blowing the roof off Ibrox at a Rangers game.

I got into the house that night completely drained. To go from the fear of thinking nobody would back what we were doing to seeing the entire stadium get behind it was just staggering. That was probably the real birth of Sons of Struth.

The conduct of the club and the lies they told about us just got worse. A couple called Gordon and Clare McLennan helped us a lot that day. After the game, they headed straight to Glasgow Airport and flew out to Dubai on holiday. The minute they arrived at their destination they contacted me. Gordon said: "Craig, you'll never guess who was on the same plane as us?" Craig Mather had been on their flight.

Now, they were on the night flight to Dubai. They touched down around lunchtime on the Sunday. But on Monday morning Mather was in the newspapers claiming he had bumped into Rangers fans in the street who told him they wouldn't be back at Ibrox until these protests ended. He said that supporters had told him their children were scared and they wouldn't be returning. But he had been on a flight to Dubai. It was absolute bunkum.

As far as I am aware, Mather didn't interact at all with Rangers fans during his time in Glasgow anyway. I heard one story about one supporter grabbing him by the throat and pinning him to the wall at a function which he attended. But that was all.

The response after the Stenhousemuir game was incredible. Our Facebook page went into meltdown. We ended up in every newspaper in the country, on the radio and even got a mention on Sky Sports. What followed after that turned my life upside down.

WHEN the media started looking for somebody from Sons of Struth to interview, Sandy Chugg had this paranoia about his past. He was worried it would detract from the message we were trying to put across. But he also had personal issues to deal with. He had lost his brother Christopher, who had been ill for a long time.

Like many people who experience the bereavement of a close family relative, he went through a period of shock immediately afterwards. I think the loss took some time to fully hit him. But when it did finally hit him it him hard.

Our initial intention was for nobody from Sons of Struth to put their name into the public domain. But some peculiar things started to happen and that quickly changed. There were lots of factors behind me becoming the person who stood in front of cameras and spoke to journalists. I would have liked to have shared responsibility. It would maybe have impacted less on my life if we had.

I was living in Houston in Renfrewshire with my girlfriend Tracy at the time. The first thing I would do every morning was go downstairs, open the back door, stand on the step, smoke a cigarette and go online on my mobile phone and read the newspapers.

One day there was a pile of ashes a couple of feet away from the bottom step. It was quite a considerable size. It was really strange.

I looked at it long and hard and racked my brains. I wondered: "Why the hell's there a pile of ashes at the back door?"

Tracy came into the kitchen and noticed it immediately too. She asked: "What's that?" I didn't want to distress her so I dismissed it. I said: "It'll just be from the barbecue. The wind will just have caught it." But it definitely wasn't. I am convinced it was a message, a warning, from somebody. To this day, I have no idea who.

It wasn't the only unsettling thing which happened. We lived in a quiet little cul-de-sac. One day I was coming back and I met our neighbour who had been out walking his dog.

He said: "Who were the guys up looking for you at four o'clock this morning?"

I replied: "What are you talking about?

"There were three transit vans here early this morning. I got up because the dog was barking. There were guys pointing at the house. Who've you upset?"

"I haven't upset anybody."

"Well, they weren't here looking for me."

It was quite worrying. I didn't know who it was. Somebody we were shouting abuse at on match days? Fans who didn't like what we were doing? Somebody whose job was under threat? Heavies who had been sent to put the frighteners on me? I don't know. It certainly wasn't as a result of anything else I had done in my life. I felt at the time it was done to scare me. It was somebody saying: "We know where you live."

I have two old friends who have associates who are, to put it delicately, slightly off-centre Glasgow businessmen. They each revealed to me independently of each other that my name was being bandied about in some fairly serious circles. By all accounts, the message being put out was: "This boy should keep his mouth shut or he'll end up getting a doing." I was told: "People have been asking questions about you. The sort of people you don't want to be getting on the wrong side of."

That made me sit up straight with a jolt. It wasn't as if I was wearing a bullet-proof vest and looking over my shoulder as I walked down the street. But I was certainly told: "People are asking about you, wanting to know where you lived." It just verified what

I suspected at the time. That certain individuals were unhappy.

I spoke to lots of people about it. The size of my contacts book probably trebled after I started Sons of Struth. I looked through it and thought: "Who's best placed to give me advice about this?" I went to people who had shown us support who were maybe familiar with a world that I had no knowledge of. The sort of blokes you could best describe as cheeky chappies.

I thought they would know the people who were making enquiries, would understand how they operated, could perhaps even vouch for me with them. By that point in time, I was starting to get requests to do interviews. I asked: "Should I go public? What can I do about these concerns I have for my personal safety?"

The message I got back was: "If you're in the public eye it would be a far bigger deal if, heaven forbid, anything was to happen to you. Therefore, it's less likely to happen. Putting yourself out there is probably an insurance policy of sorts."

Looking back now, I would say the questions which were getting asked about me seemed to stop when I started to get my face in the newspapers. People stopped digging for information on me.

I've never had any face-to-face threats. Nobody has approached me in the street and warned me off verbally. That has happened to other people. Long before I got involved, after Craig Whyte had taken over, people who had been asking serious questions about his intentions were threatened and threatened quite heavily too. It was a lot worse than anything I have ever suffered. They were approached in broad daylight as they were walking down the street and told in very plain terms what would happen to them if they continued making noises.

If it hadn't been for the intimidation we probably would have stayed a faceless movement. But the decision was made. I have spoken to people about what happened and have been asked: "Why didn't you just stop? You must have been terrified?"

I had one night when I was a bit edgy. It was a warm evening, the windows were open and there were noises outside. I was probably scared for about one hour. But, if anything, it just made me more boisterous. The way I saw it was simple. Rangers had been wronged. I wanted to shout about it.

Naively, we thought that if we staged the protest the board would realise how unpopular they were and strive to do better. They would stop telling lies and be more transparent. In hindsight, that was never going to happen.

One of the first big articles we did was in the Daily Record. Their sports journalist Scott McDermott wrote a double page spread about me in the lead-up to the AGM that year. In the course of the interview I referred to "my pal Sandy". I got a follow-up call from Scott a few days later and he asked more detailed questions about him.

I was informed by a couple of other people that Jack Irvine was attempting to remind the newspapers about Sandy's past. Not only that, I was told he was asking around if there was anything dodgy in my past. They tried to discredit us from the start.

Fortunately, I've never been in trouble with the law in my life. But what did concern me was that I was separated from the mother of my two children. The thought crossed my mind: "Will they latch onto that part of my life?" It was quite frightening to think people were trying to dig up dirt on me.

I said to Scott: "Just Google Daily Record and Sandy Chugg. The last two stories your own paper has run about him have been very positive." Anti-sectarian campaigners had spoken to Sandy about the youth football team he was coaching. They were so impressed with his commitment they ended up sponsoring the side. A nice story appeared about how this transformed character was working away for the good of his local community.

I said to Scott: "How can this guy be portrayed in such a good light six months ago, but, now he's speaking out against the Rangers board, he is being portrayed in a bad light? You can't have it both ways."

It was nonsense. When we had coached Drumsagard together I managed to get a backer for the team. I approached a retired policeman I knew who I had worked with in sales in the past. He had subsequently set up his own business and done very well. When I contacted him, he said to me straight away: "How much do you want?"

We bought strips with his money and invited him to be a guest at a fund-raising night which we held at the Halfway Bowling Club. I had to leave early for some reason and when I did Sandy took my seat next to the sponsor. I phoned him the next day to see if he had enjoyed himself. He said: "What a absolute diamond Sandy is! The funny thing is, when I was in the police I was in a surveillance team which tailed him for six months before he got busted for selling ecstasy tablets!"

I found the fact that a man who had once helped to put Sandy in jail for dealing drugs was prepared to put money into the youth football club he was then helping to run quite funny. It also showed that people can move on with their lives if you let them.

The Sunday Mail ran the story about me with a paragraph about Sandy and his past misdemeanours. But some people were trying to make him the bigger story than Sons of Struth. I hadn't dealt with the media before then. We felt what we were doing was justified. It was quite shocking to me. I am comfortable with it now. With journalists phoning me up looking for a quote. With photographers taking my picture. But to begin with it was quite surreal.

CHAPTER 5
THREE MORE TO GO!

"That's not a Brian Stockbridge lookalike!
That's Brian Stockbridge!"

Billy Montgomery, Rangers supporter.

THE Evening Times sports journalist Matthew Lindsay was one of the first reporters to write about Sons of Struth. I felt he had covered our protest at the Stenhousemuir game the most comprehensively and positively so I pinged off an email to thank him. He replied immediately asking to speak to me. I got a mutual acquaintance to vouch for him, phoned him back and we had a chat.

I thought it would be good to give Matthew something in return for his report. At that time, we were plotting an LED van stunt at Ibrox and some other famous landmarks around Glasgow so I asked him if he would be interested in doing a story on it. He set it up.

If I hadn't been getting threatened then only a photograph of the van outside the stadium and a Sons of Struth statement about what was happening at Rangers would have appeared. But I had been. So a photograph of Craig Houston standing next to the van outside the stadium and commenting on what was happening at Rangers appeared. It was the first time I had gone public.

I had pulled together some people who had been helping us for a meeting at The Ivory Hotel in Shawlands. The plan we came up with first was to project an image onto Ibrox.

At the Queen's Diamond Jubilee celebrations the year before Buckingham Palace had been lit up with a Union Jack. That is where we got the idea. One of the group suggested: "Let's beam 'SPIVS OUT'' or 'SACK THE BOARD' onto the main stand."

But there were a couple of problems. Some of the traditionalists were against it. They believed Ibrox should be sacrosanct. I myself argued: "If you can light up Buckingham Palace then surely anything goes!"

But you have to respect the views of others. So we settled on doing it on the side of the Copland Road Stand or the Broomloan Road Stand. If anything, they were probably better canvases for us to work on. Plus, it could still be seen from Edmiston Drive.

Our next problem was getting equipment strong enough to do the job and then powering it. We needed a projector, a generator, a van. It became clear there was quite a bit involved in what was essentially a silly, throwaway idea. Our hopes kept getting raised and then dashed. I must admit I got fed up with the whole thing quite quickly.

But I got a text message one morning as I was coming out of the newsagents which gave me an idea. It was an advert for an LED advertising van with moving pictures. Just as I was about to delete it, I noticed it was a number in the Hamilton area. I phoned the guy up.

Scott Campbell, my old boyhood friend from Linwood, had become a graphic designer. He was charged with producing some visual images which he duly did. We agreed a day and a time to drive the van around Ibrox and then on to Fresher's Haugh, where Rangers had been formed, and George Square with his pictures rotating on the side of the van.

Matthew was going to be on holiday at the time so he passed the story on to his colleague Chris Jack who arranged for the photographer to come up and take pictures of me next to the van outside the stadium.

Big Boris and the Ballieston True Blues paid for the van. Boris was a wealthy guy who I had known of before I got involved in the fight against the club. He was a friend of a friend. With the support he gave Sons of Struth financially and me personally throughout our campaign I became very good pals with him.

Boris called and said he wanted a couple of photographs next to it. I asked the van driver to wait for 15 or 20 minutes. He suggested: "Just for a laugh, let's drive around Ibrox a couple of times." I said: "Follow me!"

We turned off Edmiston Drive, drove behind the Broomloan Road Stand and then turned right alongside what is now The Sandy Jardine Stand. Just as I was drawing near to the front door of Argyle House this total clown steps right out in front of me. I slammed the brakes on.

I was speaking to my mate Billy Montgomery hands free on my mobile at the time. After I had stopped, he said: "What happened?"

I told him: "This Brian Stockbridge lookalike just walked in front of my car! I very nearly knocked him down!"

"Where is he now?"

"He's just walked over to his car."

"Is it a silver Mercedes coupe?"

"Aye, it is."

"That's not a Brian Stockbridge lookalike! That's Brian Stockbridge!"

I immediately jumped out of the car and Brian Stockbridge was standing there staring at the van. As luck would have it, there was a six foot photograph of him on the side of the van at that very moment next to the words: "STOCKBRIDGE NEXT!" Perfect timing.

AT that stage, I was still undecided over whether James and Sandy Easdale were fair cop or not. The slogan next to one of the pictures on the van was: "THREE MORE TO GO." It had an image of the Easdale brothers and Brian Stockbridge. I must admit I wasn't completely comfortable with it. I asked the photographer not to take a picture of it.

But I had taken some photos on my mobile along with Billy, Boris and Sandy. Inevitably, these had been forwarded to a pal, then to another mate and so on. Typically, the one photograph which hit the internet was the one of the Easdale brothers and Brian Stockbridge with "THREE MORE TO GO". Before I knew what had happened it was on a supporters' internet forum.

By all accounts, that put Sandy Easdale's nose right out of joint. It was the first time I had got a reaction from him. In fact, it created a bit of a stir. A friend of mine had a son who was in the same youth football team as Sandy's son and they stood at the side of the park watching games together. The feedback I got was that he was not best pleased. "What have I done wrong?" he asked. I was to hear that a lot from him.

Everybody else that we had a pop at was, I felt, a justifiable target. But I wasn't convinced James and Sandy Easdale, at that time, were. Before very long, things happened which made them fair game too. But at that specific moment they weren't in my opinion.

At that point, the main thing I knew about Sandy Easdale was that, many years before, he had been convicted of VAT fraud and sentenced to 27 months in prison. But campaigning against him on the basis of what he had done a long, long time before didn't really wash.

We couldn't have stood up as two fans, one of whom has criminal convictions and has served jail time, and say this man, who has criminal convictions and has served jail time, shouldn't be involved with the club. It would have been double standards. Having said that, Sandy Chugg was just a fan, a member of a supporters' protest group. He had no desire, unlike his namesake Sandy Easdale, to represent Rangers in any official capacity.

I met with Sandy Easdale on numerous occasions and spoke to him on the phone regularly. He was no different to anybody you will meet in a pub in the East End of Glasgow. Believe it or not, you could talk to him easily enough. He was the sort of bloke you could have a blether with.

But I was brought up in the traditions of Rangers, when men like Lawrence Marlborough, John Paton, John Lawrence, David Holmes and others, prominent city figures and widely-respected men with real standing in society, served on the board for the good of the club. Was Sandy Easdale what you expect from a director? The answer had to be: "No."

I encountered John Paton, the former chairman, personally on a few occasions when I went into car sales after my brief stint in the civil service. I had worked for his son Billy Paton and his business partner Billy Peterkin, who sadly passed away after a tragic accident on his stag weekend in Spain many years later, at a garage in Paisley for a spell.

They had a boardroom situated at the back of the showroom. The employees used to sneak in there and eat our sandwiches at lunch. One day I ran in there in a hurry - you always seemed to be in a rush in the motor trade - and opened up my sandwiches and my can of juice.

Then out of the corner of my eye I caught John Paton sitting in the chairman's seat at the end of the table. I got a fright. "Sorry Mr Paton!" I exclaimed. "I'll go!"

He said: "No, son, you support the Rangers don't you? Stay and tell me about the game on Saturday. I'm having my lunch as well."

So that was what we did. At that time, you almost bowed down to somebody who was an ex-Rangers chairman. He was a lovely man, as was his son.

I had heard about the Easdale brothers many years before. When I left school a lot of boys of my age went to work in factories in the Inverclyde area where their business empire was based. There were urban myths about them. The best way of describing them is "a well-known family".

Oddly enough, I had encountered them elsewhere too. My son had played for a couple of seasons with Queen's Park youth team. One night another father whose son was on trial with the club appeared in a huge expensive car. He sported what I would call a wealthy streetwise look about him. It was Sandy Easdale.

He wasn't Rangers director material for me. Yes, he was a businessman. But he had worked in the licensed trade, had owned scrap yards and had run private hire taxi firms. He hadn't been within a mile of a PLC boardroom in his life.

He had done well to get from where he started in his life. You should be able to start from humble beginnings and better yourself. Even taking away the criminal conviction, though, he wasn't what you were looking for in the board room at Ibrox.

The odd thing was, out of all the current and former directors I met in the course of the journey I went on, Sandy Easdale was probably the one who had most in common with me as a person. It was bizarre because he was, so to speak, the enemy. We would get on fine if we met in different circumstances. We are from the same sort of backgrounds. We talk in the same language. We are similar characters. We speak our minds. But he just didn't do what was the best for Rangers in my opinion.

Blue Pitch Holdings, an investment group whose financiers' identity was unknown, had requisitioned an EGM in May to remove Malcolm Murray and Phil Cartmell and replace them with James Easdale and their agent Chris Morgan.

After a few weeks Murray and Cartmell eventually departed along with the nominated advisor Cenkos and Easdale was appointed. A club announcement to the Stock Exchange confirmed the new director only owned a 0.5 per cent shareholding.

However, the stake his brother Sandy held along with the proxies for Blue Pitch Holdings and Margarita Holdings Trust, meant the faction the majority of the supporters was opposed to now effectively controlled the club.

Frank Blin and Paul Murray attempted to strike a compromise with the board in order to avoid the necessity for an EGM. They believed they had managed to reach an agreement which would have seen Blin, Paul Murray, Sandy Easdale and former chairman John McLelland appointed to the board.

On the day an announcement to the Stock Exchange was due the new nominated advisor Strand Hanson blocked it. No reasons were given. Blin withdrew from the process and non-executive director Ian Hart resigned as the stand-off became increasingly acrimonious and public.

The McColl camp regrouped and by the end of September it emerged Scott Murdoch, Malcolm Murray, Paul Murray and Alex Wilson had been put forward for election to the Rangers board at the AGM which had been called on October 24.

The club claimed it was "not valid" and blocked it. A petition for an interdict with the Court of Session in Edinburgh was promptly filed by The Requisitioners, as they became known, to prevent the meeting from going ahead without the appointment of new directors included in the business.

In an act of desperation, Mather and Stockbridge had flown to South Africa to meet Dave King, the multi-millionaire Scottish businessman and former club director who had reached a settlement with the authorities after a long-running dispute over a tax bill there and was free to invest, and offered him the position of club chairman.

The Requisitioners were handed an interim interdict to block the AGM after Lord Tyre ruled there was "no valid legal reason" for their motion not to be presented to shareholders. Mather and non-executive director Smart resigned. That left just two directors, James Easdale and Brian Stockbridge. The board, what remained of it, appeared to be in a precarious position.

I was looking at Sons of Struth Facebook page during a Rangers game one day and there were two personal messages on it telling me of an internet rumour that Sons of Struth were Malcolm Murray. Then I got a text from a friend saying that he was having on online argument with somebody who claimed Malcolm Murray ran the Sons of Struth. At this point, I had never met the man.

I just laughed about it. I met Sandy Chugg after the game and as we were walking to his car I showed him the text. We had a good chuckle about the online rumpus. That very second Sandy's phone goes. It was a call from somebody saying that Malcolm Murray wanted to meet us at the Louden Tavern.

He had been in the pub, our names were mentioned and he said: "I'd like to speak to them." It was spooky. Anyway, we went down and spoke for about quarter of an hour and told him what we were all about. I think he wanted to check us out.

He asked me: "What do you want out of this?"

I said: "I want to sit in the seat I have sat in for 32 years and look at the directors' box and say: 'I am happy with them'. I want to watch the team without my stomach churning at the thought of who is representing us on the board."

"Well, it's heartening to hear there is no ulterior motive."

He asked how he could get in contact with us. As time went on in the build-up to the AGM we got quite heavily involved with him.

There were two distinct sides to his personality. One was his professional side. Then there was the Rangers fan. He was very business-orientated and well-connected in the city. But he was a Rangers supporter through and through as well. The earliest indication I got of this was when I was having a conversation with him on the phone one night.

He said: "I'm up in the woods beside my house walking my dog. It is good sometimes to get up here and clear my head." So we carried on chatting for a few minutes. Then he said: "Hold on Craig, the dog's got away." All I hear then is him shouting: "Baxter! Baxter! Come here! Baxter!" I burst out laughing. He had named his dog after Jim Baxter.

He wasn't kidding on. He wasn't a Morton fan pretending to be a Rangers fan. He also had a young daughter who was every bit as passionate about the club as he was. He would sit in the pub talking about Rangers for an hour after the game.

DAVE King came over to Scotland to hold talks with Rangers in October. He met with the board and attended the game as their guest. The club was stalling over the date of the AGM. We knew they were doing this so they could position themselves in a better place to remain in power. So we travelled up to Methil for the game against East Fife with "AGM NOW" banners.

We would have a meeting on a Monday about a Saturday protest. But we would only order the banners on the Friday morning. Everything changed so much at the time. A week was a long time in Rangers at that time.

That was true even with the blue and red card displays. The text for those cards was only finalised the day before. Things were just so fast moving. We weren't that clever. People thought we were trying to drive the share price down and put the club on the brink of administration so somebody could come in and buy it. But the reality is we were just punters who reacted to developments as they happened.

We got a banner made up that read: "SONS OF STRUTH SAY AGM NOW". The idea was that we would get photographs done of Malcolm Murray and Scott Murdoch sitting among the fans with banners. We also planned to hold it up in front of the directors' box as they were taking their seats after half-time.

I spotted Willie Vass, a freelance photographer who covered every Rangers game for the national newspapers who, at this point, I did not know, sitting by the corner flag. I went down and said: "Do you fancy a picture nobody else will get?"

At half-time Sandy and I went and stood next to the tunnel and by pure luck Stevie Sinclair, a wheelchair fan who I had got to know after starting up Sons of Struth, was there too. I went up for a chat and said: "We're going to pull a banner out in front of Dave King and the directors. Do you mind speaking to us while we're waiting?" He said: "Aye, carry on."

While we were waiting, the Rangers substitutes were warming up. A boy comes up and says: "Can I squeeze past you? I'm wanting to get my picture taken with David Templeton." Davie was standing six feet away signing autographs. Davie used to come along and coach the kids at Drumsagard Academy when he played for Hearts. Sandy had known a schoolfriend of his and arranged it.

We had heard a rumour that he was wanting a transfer at the time.

Sandy said: "Davie, this boy's wanting a photograph with you. And what's this shite I hear about you putting in a transfer request?"

David laughed: "Shut it Sandy!"

The boy said: "Are you Sandy Chugg? Can I get a photo with you too?" He ended up getting photos with both of us. Fame at last!

We eventually got moved on by the police. But midway through the second half we wandered down and held up the banner in front of the directors' box. I knew two people who were sitting with the board that day and it got back to us that some less than complimentary remarks were made as we were passing. "What are these arseholes doing now?" was one.

The Requisitioners eventually agreed to hold the vote at the AGM on December 19 to save the club the expense of staging an EGM. But that allowed the board to bring in David Somers as chairman, Graham Wallace, the former Manchester City chief operations officer, as chief executive and Norman Crighton as a non-executive director. It increased their credibility with shareholders.

CHAPTER 6

LONDON CALLING

"I have known Laxey since they were founded."

Norman Crighton, Rangers non-executive director.

MALCOLM Murray thought it would be a good idea for me to travel to London before the Rangers AGM so I got the sleeper down one night in November.

I wanted to get a better understanding of what the major institutional investors were thinking. I was keen to tell them: "I'm a fan and we don't like the current board." I was eager, too, to drum up some support for The Requisitioners among the shareholders.

Sky Sports News had asked to interview me as well. It was at the same time as Bernie Ecclestone, the Formula One boss, was going through a major legal case. I met their reporter Amy Lewis outside the High Court where she was covering the story and we went around the corner to film.

That was quite a big deal for the Sons of Struth. We had done bits and pieces on BBC Scotland and STV before that. But to go national with Sky Sports News was a big step up for us. The satellite broadcaster ended up running three or four pieces with us during the course of one afternoon.

Amy had arranged to meet her boyfriend in a nearby bar after the interview. So I tagged along with her for a drink. Just a couple of minutes after getting there my ugly mug appeared on the television screen in the pub. It was quite a strange sensation standing having a pint watching myself prattle on.

I had actually made my television debut many years before when Graeme Souness resigned as Rangers manager in 1991. I was working at the Ibrox Trophy House which my father ran on

Paisley Road West and heard he was going to quit as manager. I thought: "He can't do that! We're close to winning this league!"

I nipped out and walked up to the back to the stadium to try and find out what was happening. They sneaked him out another entrance. Nevertheless, I was glad I went up because I got to hear the full story. He wanted to stay for the remainder of the season and then move on to Liverpool. But he was told he had to go there and then. I believed the club had done the right thing.

Chick Young was there interviewing supporters for BBC Scotland and was speaking to the guy standing next to me. This lad said: "I wish Graeme all the best. I'm heartbroken he's left. I hope he does well." In my opinion, he was talking absolute garbage. I was looking at him open-mouthed as he spoke. When he had finished I said to him: "You don't half talk some amount of shite!"

Chick said: "Have you got a different opinion to him? Promise not to swear and you can do an interview for the television." My own view was that nobody was bigger than the club. Souness had fallen out with Terry Butcher, Graham Roberts and Chris Woods during his time in charge and he told them all that. Then all of sudden he declares: "I'm going to leave and join Liverpool. But I'll wait until the end of the season." I thought: "How dare you!" He had been fantastic for Rangers. But that wasn't on in my mind. Anyway, I ended up on Reporting Scotland.

MEMBERS of the London branch of the Rangers Supporters Association had started to contact me as the AGM drew nearer. They were keen to get involved in some capacity in what we were doing. So I held a meeting with their representatives.

I told them: "You're very well placed to help us." About 70 to 80 per cent of Rangers was controlled or owned by people who worked within a square mile in the City of London. They had members who worked alongside them in financial circles, in banks and for institutional investors. They were well connected.

We discussed the possibility of doing protests outside the offices of Laxey Partners or the nominated advisor Daniel Stewart. On the back of those talks, they went away and set up a meeting with Colin Kingsnorth, the founding partner of Laxey.

I met Alex Wilson for the first time at that meeting and my

impressions were favourable. He was a real straight talker. He had a similar working class background to me and I found him easy to speak to. Basically, he was a normal Rangers fan who had done well for himself. I believed he had an awful lot to offer his club as a director. He has worked for a lot of multinational companies at a high level. Rangers would have been a walk in the park for him.

A strange thing happened that day as Malcolm and I walked through the streets of the financial district. As we were making our way through a lane he stopped outside a pub called Harry's Bar. He told me: "There are probably more business deals done in there outwith office hours than there are during the day. That's where all of the high flyers meet up."

Before I knew it, the street was filled with people trying to speak to him. They had spotted him through the windows as they sat in the bar and dashed out to have a word. It was at that point that I realised the extensive contacts and considerable influence he had in the city. It was a good indication for me of the major role that he played in the success of the IPO when he was Rangers chairman.

They started to pump him for information. What's happening with the AGM? Will you get these guys out? What are you going to do if you get in? It became apparent to me that all of these people, shrewd businessmen and highly-paid financiers, had invested in Rangers because of Malcolm Murray not Charles Green.

A pension fund manager with over 30 years of experience, he had stewardship of 25 per cent of the shareholding of Manchester United at one point in his career. I think Green and his associates wanted him on board to lend credibility to them and their share issue. But once they had raised over £22 million it was a different story. They didn't want him involved.

None of the investors were Scottish. They bought into Rangers because Malcolm had told them it was worthwhile and because he was there to protect their money. But he was prevented from taking part in the business affairs of the club after the share offering and was gradually discredited and marginalised using some fairly unsavoury methods.

That process led to Malcolm being filmed by the financial director Brian Stockbridge as he was helped out of a restaurant. The video was eventually put online by somebody else. He was portrayed as a drunkard. The reality was he had been involved in a car accident earlier in his life, had a metal plate in his head and took medication. Even a couple of drinks had a profound effect on him.

The way he was set up was appalling. He was kept waiting in the restaurant for two or three hours ahead of a meeting. He had nothing to eat, hadn't taken his tablets and kept getting glasses of red wine thrust into his hand. Then they turned up and filmed him. He was later ousted as chairman.

A Rangers director had lost his position before after being filmed. Donald Findlay, a well-known QC, resigned as vice-chairman after being filmed singing sectarian songs at a function thrown to celebrate the Scottish Cup final win over Celtic in 1999. For me, the comparisons between what the two men did are non-existent.

A lot of fans made up their minds about Malcolm Murray because of the circumstances that he left the club under. That is what they based their opinion of him on. But after spending a great deal of time in his company I realised there was far more to him.

LAXEY Partners had initially stated they would vote with the Rangers fans at the AGM. Then, all of a sudden, they started saying they were receiving mixed messages from the supporters. It appeared somebody was feeding them false information and spinning them a line about the existing board which had no basis in reality.

Colin Kingsnorth put out a statement which implied the Rangers fans were divided and some of them were supportive of the directors. Now, I have no doubt some of them were. But if you had polled 100 of them then you would be lucky to find 10 who were of that opinion.

So we believed our meeting with Laxey, the major shareholders who owned a 12 per cent stake in the club, could be important. We hoped we could highlight how unhappy the majority of the fans were. But, unusually for somebody who had been portrayed as a media whore, an attention seeker and an ego maniac by so many, I didn't attend myself.

I pulled together a gathering of around a dozen or so people in Glasgow who I felt would be better going. I told them what was happening and asked them all to nominate two people to attend. I myself suggested that Chris Graham and Gordon Dinnie should go.

Chris was a very good speaker and had a financial background. Gordon was used to dealing with people at board meetings. Just about everyone in attendance agreed with me. They were better placed than I was to drive home our point.

But the meeting turned out to be pointless. By all accounts, Kingsnorth was abrupt and aloof. He insisted he knew nothing about the appointment of Norman Crighton as a non-executive director. It later transpired that he was their man on the board.

Indeed, Crighton himself confirmed to shareholders at the AGM that Laxey had recommended him to the nominated advisor. He said: "I have known Laxey since they were founded."

The feedback we received afterwards was that nothing the Rangers supporters had said at the meeting would have mattered. They got the impression he couldn't have cared less. There was no point in holding talks with him. There was no way his opinion was going to be changed.

Laxey 's involvement with Rangers always struck me as being slightly strange. When it had been announced during the summer that Charles Green was severing his ties with the club a statement which was put out read that he would be selling the vast majority of his shares to Sandy Easdale - apart from those he was transferring to Laxey Partners. Two different words were used. Selling and transferring.

Despite asking many knowledgeable people on many occasions, nobody has ever been able to tell us how much, if anything at all, he transferred his shares to Laxey for. I personally believe he did so for nothing. I think he did so to repay them for their investment before the share offering.

Rumour had it that Laxey, and many other investors, were promised shares at £1 a share. So if they put in £1 million they were expecting one million shares in return. But the opening price turned out to be 70p. If you do the arithmetic, the transfer of shares makes up for what they would have lost for their pre-IPO investment.

I am quite sure there will be instances of investors being paid money from Rangers who had been guaranteed by Charles Green that they would not lose money if they put money in pre-IPO.

A company called Eurovestec invested £1 million. Documents were leaked which showed they actually got £300,000 paid back.

Two direct debits of charge payments went back to them, one into a business account and one to a private account. When you added it up it totalled, unsurprisingly, £300,000. But you can't find that in the Rangers accounts.

We've never been told where the £6.5 million IPO costs went. It should have been - and it was stated quite clearly in the prospectus - £2 million. Brian Stockbridge's explanation was that it was because Rangers was a high-risk company at the time. Well, we were a high-risk company beforehand. It didn't happen overnight. These things should have been factored in.

The £6.5 million was a recurring theme. The fans were told they would be given a detailed breakdown of where the IPO costs went at the gathering at Ibrox which I wasn't able to attend. The people running Rangers would say they would do something, buy themselves some time and then stall. The vast majority of fans forgot we had been told we would get access to a detailed breakdown of those costs.

The directors probably didn't understand when fans complained: "You aren't being transparent." They probably believed that they were. They probably thought: "Well, we threw out some figures at the AGM, that'll keep them happy."

Laxey were a hedge fund. They like to get in about businesses and look at their assets, split things up and do whatever they have to do to generate pounds, shilling and pence on their balance sheet. No fan in their right mind would want a hedge fund anywhere near their club.

I'm quite sure that Laxey's kick back was what was termed as the "transfer" of shares from Charles Green. Perhaps the fact that they ended up with somebody on the board is why they did a 180 degree U-Turn on the way they voted at the AGM. They said one thing in the weeks leading up to it and suddenly changed their mind and did another.

Unfortunately, Laxey is the type of business that Charles Green attracted into the IPO. It wasn't Malcolm Murray who enticed Blue Pitch, Laxey or Margarita to the table. He brought in Artemis, Hargreave Hale, River and Mercantile, the more traditional investors. They are the ones I met in London.

My role was to tell them that, contrary to what they were hearing, the board didn't have the backing of the supporters. When they heard that Laxey had changed their minds they felt that perhaps the fans weren't against the board. I wanted to tell them that wasn't the truth. I wanted to show them the protests we had been involved in. I wanted to show them: "This is a red card protest. That is how the supporters feel."

We were getting well covered by the media in Scotland. But I feared that publicity wouldn't have filtered down to these individuals, apart from those who had been born in Scotland and had moved down there to work, and they would be none the wiser. We wanted to show them the information they had been drip fed by the club was false. I went down there to say: "I am a fan. This is the group we have started. We want these guys out."

I also asked them to come to the AGM. Now, I didn't think the reaction to the board would have been as hostile. But those who made the trip certainly knew, the minute they got there, how the fans felt.

I met them on their lunch breaks and after work. I don't think I persuaded anybody who was going to vote for the board to vote for The Requisitioners. I think most of them were going to vote that way as it was. But I do think it made a difference and helped to cement their views. Certainly, nobody I met and spoke to voted for the board.

It was bizarre trip. One minute I am standing outside the High Court in London being interviewed by a Sky Sports presenter I had seen on television speaking to famous footballers. The next thing I am watching myself on television. Then I am meeting up with a potential director. Then I am talking to representatives of institutional investors who have put millions of pounds into the club.

They were more of those moments where I felt like it was not me standing there. It was like I was standing on the shoulders of somebody else. I felt a fan of a football club shouldn't be in the position to be doing these things.

We were always trying to figure out what our opposition was going to do. I thought to myself: "Why don't they just have the AGM?" I thought it was quite evident they would be beaten. I asked: "What are they going to pull out of the hat?" They put Crighton, Somers and Wallace onto the board and talked up their track records.

We staged a banner protest at Murray Park in the month of the AGM. It was to show to the team that although we were going to turn up and start bawling and shouting again we weren't against them in any way. Indeed, the slogan for that protest was: "Back the team not the regime."

We thought on Friday there would be plenty of reporters and camera crews there. A few of them came out and interviewed us. The cameras took lots of pictures of us. The players all saw it.

Then somebody came out and told us that Ally McCoist would be quite keen to have a word with us if we could hold on. Eventually he appeared. He stopped his car and got out to chat. He signed some autographs and had some photos taken. The gist of his message to us was: "I get what you are doing. You are allowed your opinion. The players know it is nothing to do with them and they understood that at the Stenhousemuir and East Fife games. They know it is purely to do with the regime."

That was what we wanted to achieve. We didn't want our actions to be affecting the team in any way. And I honestly don't think they did. In the first protest we staged we triumphed 8-0. We won every game we staged a major demonstration at.

Some people took exception to what we were doing. They said: "You aren't getting behind the team. What you are doing will affect the team." Well, that wasn't the case. It was one of the reasons we came up with the format - in the 18th and 72nd minutes - for our protests.

Ally was a Rangers fan before he was a Rangers player before he was the Rangers manager. He stood on the terraces as a boy. Regardless of how results went and how his career as manager panned out, he will always retain the connection he has with the fans. He is held in high regard for what he has done in the past. He has always been great with the fans as well.

When the players came out we would say to them: "Can you see what the banner says?" We made sure they knew what we were doing was nothing to do with them and outlined what we were going to do at the game the following day. They were all comfortable with it.

A couple of the staff came out and told us: "Keep doing what you're doing! We're on your side!" I dare say a few of their colleagues weren't of the same opinion. But nobody said to us. We received lots of messages of support from club workers on that occasion and on many others before and after as well.

THE public meeting with all four of the Requisitioners and their supporter Jim McColl in the Grosvenor Hilton Hotel at the end of November was an idea the boys who regularly got together to help Sons of Struth plan the protests came up with.

Simon Leslie, who does a lot of DJing and compering of Rangers events, took it upon himself to organise it and booked a function suite. Sie had been actively involved in our activities and had helped to arrange banners for the first demonstration.

Simon attempted to contact the Rangers directors to invite them. I got an email from Jack Irvine one day asking me about the meeting. I passed on the details of who was going to be in attendance and what would be discussed. The answer I received back was: "Well, the board won't be going."

I spoke to Sandy Easdale about it afterwards. He was adamant he would have liked to have been there. He told me he was in the West End of Glasgow on the night and was actually considering popping along. I would have liked to have seen that. It would have been entertaining.

One of the best photographs to come out of that night was of the top table. We had the names of the four Requisitioners alongside the names of the board members who failed to turn up. It was quite a nice visual image.

On numerous occasions in the run-up to the AGM Frank Blin and Paul Murray had both felt they were about to be manoeuvred into places the board at Ibrox. But every time they had they were turned down at the last minute. The board would blame the nominated advisor. The nominated advisor would blame somebody else. And on and on it went.

I experienced that situation myself. I was in discussions with directors along with others and we all felt we were on the verge of getting an agreement on something. Then a day later they backtracked completely and we were back to square one.

You could tell by the questions at the public meeting whether the person was pro-board or anti-board. Inevitably, there were some really stupid points made. One lad, for example, wanted to know if Paul Murray had been responsible for getting The Billy Boys banned when he was a director. But there were some good, difficult, in-your-face questions. It was exactly what we wanted.

At the end of the night I asked my fellow organisers: "Did those guys have more people supporting them when they walked out of that meeting than when they walked in?" The consensus of opinion among the people I spoke to was: "Yes, they did."

If it was down to the Rangers supporters those four people would have become directors. Unfortunately, we were a PLC.

CHAPTER 7

ADVENTURES IN CYBERSPACE

"You're still an arsehole, but you have to know what's just happened. There's something not right with your phone."

Sandy Chugg, Sons of Struth co-founder.

IN the build-up to the public meeting with The Requisitioners at the Hilton Grosvenor Hotel at the end of November, an email account the Rangers supporters organising the event had set up was hacked.

We were limited to 500 people at the venue. On the off chance more than that turned up on the night, we opened an email account to determine the numbers that would appear. We asked people who planned to attend to register their interest.

A couple of lassies volunteered to help us with the administration for the evening. They started drawing up a list of names so that when people came in we could tick them off. They noticed the email account had been hacked twice in the run-up to the event. Thankfully, most of the names had been saved elsewhere.

It was obvious, though, that somebody, somewhere was determined to create difficulties for us. It could have been anybody. It could have been Celtic fans making mischief. It could have been Rangers supporters who were pro-board. But my intuition told me it was people working on behalf of the board or on behalf of certain shareholders who were opposed to the meeting and those involved in it.

Exactly the same thing happened to me later on. I opened my email inbox one day and there were 54 messages in it. I went back in a few hours later and there were just two. Somebody had gone in and deleted them all. I lost a lot of important information as a result.

It also happened when the Sons of Struth were arranging a march on Ibrox with the aim of safeguarding the stadium the following year. We needed people to volunteer to be stewards so that it satisfied legal requirements. An email account I had set up for that was hacked and data which had been collated was corrupted.

I had to prove to Glasgow City Council I had 300 marshalls for the march in order for it to go ahead. I created a website and had a section on it for people to register their interest via an email account I had set up. That way I could draw up a list to show the council. Every day I would check it and pretty soon I was comfortable we would have the necessary number of helpers for the march to go ahead.

I had a meeting arranged with council officials on the Monday morning and logged in to the email account on the Sunday night with the intention of setting up a spread sheet to show them. Somebody had deleted everything. It was a completely separate account from the one I had experienced problems with before.

Shortly after the AGM there was more cyber skullduggery. I was driving home from work one afternoon and Paul Murray phoned me.

He said: "Craig, what are these emails you've sent me all about? They don't make any sense!"

I told him: "Paul, I've not emailed you in a long time. And I've not emailed anybody at all today."

"Well, I've got three emails from you."

Straight away, I thought: "Somebody's hacked into my email address."

When I got home I started up my laptop and went into my emails. I looked in the sent box fully expecting to see three messages which had been forwarded. But there was nothing. I called Paul back and asked him to tell me what exact email address he had received the messages from. My email address was sonsofstruth@aol.co.uk. The email address he had received a message from was sonsofsrtuth@aol.co.uk. Somebody had created an email address and swapped the t with the r in so it read like my email address at a glance.

The emails Paul received were suggesting we had done something illegal.

They said things like: "Paul, what do you want me to do with the information we spoke about."

He had replied: "What are you talking about Craig?"

The message came back: "That thing we talked about."

They were clearly trying to get him to divulge something. Unfortunately for them, there was no information because nothing untoward had gone on.

But I realised that anybody I had been in contact with throughout the whole Sons of Struth campaign, from ordinary supporters to MPs, could have been contacted by somebody pretending to be me. That was unsettling. I took it to somebody I knew in the police and asked them to look into it. They did so and suggested charging the person responsible with breach of the peace.

Within 24 hours I had the two postal addresses where the emails had been sent from. When you send any email, there is a header on it you don't see. It is just a row of digits, letters and symbols. But computer experts can use those details to determine exactly where an email has originated from.

A chap who had been involved with the protests helped us out on that front. He told us it was possible to pinpoint a street name from an email and came back with the addresses for two private residences. One was from a working class area of Glasgow and one was from an affluent area of East Kilbride.

We ascertained from there that it was two members of another Rangers supporters' group who had been responsible.

The police eventually told us no criminality had been involved so no further action could be taken. There was nothing to stop somebody opening up an email account titled craighouston@sonsofsrtuth.com. Even if their name wasn't Craig Houston and they had nothing to do with Sons of Struth. It was unnerving. But it was more annoying than anything. Somebody sitting in their spare room in front of a computer doesn't scare me in the same way a face-to-face physical threat would.

But getting involved in a fight with fellow Rangers fans was of no interest to me so I decided not to approach and confront them.

Some Rangers fans' groups didn't actively support what we were doing. The Vanguard Bears, for example, is a group that has done a lot of good things in the past. For example, they raised money to build a headstone for William McBeath, one of the founding fathers of Rangers who was buried in a pauper's grave. I don't have any issues with them. Their aims are not purely to do with football. I have spoken to guys who are in the organisation's hierarchy in the past and found them to be cracking lads.

The problem was with people at the bottom end of their organisation who spent their lives on the internet. It is a strange body in as much as if you were to ask somebody straight out if they were a member they would retreat into their shell. You would be treated with suspicion for even asking them. They are highly secretive. It is a lot of nonsense if you ask me. The main players in the organisation will happily go on television to get interviewed wearing Vanguard Bears polo shirts. But some won't even confirm if they are members.

The Vanguard Bears are good at what they do online. They are almost on a par with Celtic supporters in that area. I switched on the television to watch a Celtic Champions League qualifier one night. The first thing I saw was a player taking a throw in. Behind him in the crowd was a fan holding a green and white saltire with "Vote Yes" written on it in support of Scottish Independence. Now, that isn't allowed. UEFA guidelines stipulate that you aren't allowed political banners at football matches.

I saw it - along with, no doubt, thousands of other Rangers fans who were watching in the hope that Celtic got beat - but nothing came of it. If that had happened at a Rangers game, if one of our fans had been spotted with a Union Flag with "Vote No" on it, there would, without question, have been a thousand emails sent to UEFA before the final whistle.

The Celtic supporters, to be fair to them, seem to mobilise online far quicker than Rangers fans. They use social media effectively and appreciate the value of it.

But the Vanguard Bears are also good at campaigning online. I can remember a story breaking about a guy from East Kilbride who claimed his dog had been subjected to sectarian abuse and attacked by Rangers fans because it had been wearing a Celtic strip. The guy was, not surprisingly, a complete rocket. Within hours, the Vanguard Bears had dug up a lot of information about the individual and shown he wasn't the innocent victim he was attempting to make out.

But the ones at the bottom of the ladder, who may not actually even be Vanguard Bears, are just a pain. They are malicious. According to some of them, I am a Celtic supporter. In fact, some claimed I even went to Barcelona to watch "my team" play in the Champions League.

I don't normally let the online stuff bother me. But one of the most disgusting things which happened to me throughout this campaign happened in cyberspace. I was getting ready to go to bed one night and a message popped up on my Facebook from a member of the London branch of the Rangers Supporters Association. It read: "Craig, have you seen the post about you on Twitter? You'd better check it out."

Somebody called @BladeGer had posted a screen grab of a Sons of Struth Facebook page with jokes about the Ibrox disaster and people in wheelchairs on it. At first glance, I thought it was some sort of tasteless dig at Sir David Murray. But there were references to Daleks having difficulty getting up stairs. I thought: "Nobody would be sick enough to write about the Ibrox Disaster and pretend it was me."

I had to read it twice. After I did, I broke out in a cold sweat. I panicked. Anybody who knew me would realise what it was and know I would never post anything like that. But there are thousands of people on social media who wouldn't know that.

It transpired that you can create a fake Facebook post online. There is a website where you can put somebody else's details in and it will make it look as if they have posted something. It can replicate their photograph and everything. Then the person just does a screen grab and posts that. It looks genuine.

I sent a message to the guy who had posted it expressing my anger and disgust. I then made up a fake Facebook post myself and wrote: "This is how easy it is to do what this idiot's done." The level of support I received over that was gratifying. It wasn't just from people who were anti-board either. There were people who were pretty vile to me online who were expressing their disgust. Hopefully, I caught it quick enough to stop any damage.

I was born after the Ibrox Disaster. But as a Rangers supporter it is something which is ingrained in me. I can remember going to the 40th anniversary service in 2011. I was as upset about that as I had been at any family member's funeral. It is chilling because I have stood on terraces at Ibrox cheering on my team myself just like the 66 people who lost their lives in 1971. Nobody should go to a football match and not return home.

I get emotional whenever I go to a match in January. I am unable to walk past the John Greig statue in front of the main stand without thinking about it. So for somebody to make up a fake Facebook post in my name which showed me making derogatory remarks about the Ibrox Disaster was difficult to take. I felt physically ill.

On the day of the Hillsborough Disaster in 1989 Rangers had been playing at Parkhead in a Scottish Cup semi-final. My dad and I came out of the ground and were walking back to the car when we heard there had been crowd trouble at the FA Cup semi-final and people had been hurt. English football had a bad reputation at the time.

When we got into the car we switched on the radio and the full horror or what happened hit us. First we heard that 10 people were dead. Then it was 20. Then it was 30. Eventually the death toll was up in the 80s and 90s. It was a horrible.

My father had been at Ibrox on the day of the Ibrox Disaster so it was especially shocking for him. But I think that is true of any Rangers supporter. As I said, it is in your blood. Seeing fans of another club going through the same thing was terrible. I can honestly not recall what the score that day was or who the opposition were.

I can remember going to the 40th anniversary of the Ibrox Disaster and a big flag came out for Rangers and Liverpool, for the 66 and the 96. There is a Hillsborough/Ibrox Memorial Group. I don't know anybody who was hurt or who died at it. But it still stirs the emotions.

There were other sinister events which left me cold. Sandy Chugg and I are more akin to brothers than pals. We have daft arguments and go in the huff with each other. But we usually make up and get back on speaking terms pretty quickly.

But Sandy was going through some serious personal difficulties after we started up and said some things which were very personal and hurtful to me. I responded in a similar manner. It was all just said in the heat of an argument. He was in a bad place at the time and I was under pressure too. Deep down, I knew that, despite how aggrieved I was, and I was certain he was the same.

But if you had been listening as an outside party your ears may have pricked up at what was said. We didn't talk to each other for a couple of weeks after what was quite a heated dispute.

I had harboured serious concerns about my iPhone being tapped for some time before this. When I was calling certain numbers there would be a long pause before I would get connected. I would hear clicking noises in the background when I was having a conversation. My signal would suddenly half in strength for no reason.

I went on to the internet to see what the telltale signs that your phone was being tapped were. It turned out I was experiencing all of them. I also discovered that it is fairly easy to access information contained on an iPhone from a laptop if you know how. Once you have done that you can see all of the text messages, listen to voice mails and read emails. You can access virtually anything.

An iPhone also has a four digit code to unlock it which is time sensitive. If you haven't used your phone for a certain amount of time you have to type in your number to open it. After a while, doing that becomes second nature to you. You hardly give doing it a second thought.

Somebody asked me one day if I had a code for my iPhone. I told them I did. Then I thought: 'Hold on a minute! It's not on. I haven't put my code in for months now.' I went into the settings and the lock had been switched off.

Apparently, the first time somebody has managed to obtain access to your data via their laptop the first thing they do is go into the settings and turn off the lock. That means they can get in at any stage in the future.

My security lock being off was another indicator my device had been tampered with. I certainly hadn't done it. Why would I? It had so much sensitive information and so many important phone numbers for directors, managers and former players contained on it. I was obviously keen for it to remain private.

Anyway, Sandy had said some highly personal things to me when we were arguing on the phone. Within an hour of us hanging up on each other like a pair of petulant schoolboys he received a call from somebody, who would not give his name, relaying exactly what he had said to me. He was told he could quite easily get that information to a journalist and into the newspapers.

Sandy told him where to go and called me straight back. He said: "Look, you're still an arsehole, but you have to know what's just happened. There's something not right with your phone."

THE online Rangers community can be appalling. I imagine supporters of other clubs feel the same about their fans at times. But I am doubtful they plumb the same sort of depths some of the followers of my club unfortunately do.

I appreciate that when the final whistle blows at a game at Ibrox no two Rangers fans in the crowd will have the same opinion about the goalkeeper, the right back or the referee. In the real world, you will stand in a bar and talk quite civilly to somebody who disagrees with your view of the centre forward, opposition team or manager. But online the debate is poisonous for some reason.

I had people send me messages that said: "Hoi you ya bastard! You're trying to ruin our fucking club!" Then they would ask you a question. It made me scratch my head. Nobody in everyday life would come up to you, give you a torrent of abuse and then immediately ask for your thoughts on a variety of different topics. It was downright bizarre.

When somebody disagreed with them they would say: "Oh aye, you must be a Tim!" But no two Rangers fans agree on everything about their club. Sandy and I formed Sons of Struth together and are as tight as two brothers. But even we didn't agree all the time about things concerning our club. Surely you have to accept that people have different views?

The other camp was: "You don't talk for me! How dare you say this! How dare you say that!" Of course I didn't! I never once conducted a newspaper, radio or television interview and said: "I am speaking on behalf of every Rangers fan here." No, I was speaking on behalf of Sons of Struth and I would say whatever I wanted.

I told them: "If you have a different opinion then you go and speak to the newspapers, radio or television." They would reply: "But nobody knows me!" I responded: "Well, nobody knew me. But I got up off my backside and went and did something about it. I shouted about my unhappiness about what was going on at the club I loved because I cared so much." Sorry, but nobody was going to make me feel like a bad person for taking action.

One of the most unpleasant places to go onto was Twitter. It was just rancid. The reason for that was that not many people post under their actual name. They hide behind false identities. It struck me that the more bizarre the title - and there are people named after majors at the Battle of the Boyne in 1690 - the greater sense of entitlement they feel to voice an opinion on the club. If you are @DukeofSchomborg you are more of a Rangers fan than @SonsofStruth apparently.

I used to go on Twitter and try to debate points intelligently. But it would just descend into a torrent of abuse. The folk who attack you are proper dafties. It is the same clique of people as well. You do get drawn in. I started thinking: "What am I doing?" Eventually I set it up so anything I posted on Facebook automatically went up on Twitter so I didn't have to go on it.

One of the most high-profile threats to me was made on Rangers Media, an internet forum that did not have many, if any, Sons of Struth supporters posting on it.

When I did one of my first interviews with Scott McDermott from the Daily Record he wrote that I was from Linwood. Now, technically I was. I had been brought up there. But I was living in Houston at that time with my then girlfriend. I wanted to keep that quiet. It suited me for nobody to know where I stayed given the threats I had received.

As a result of the Daily Record article, the perception started that I lived in Linwood and I was quite happy about that. It meant that if anybody was of a mind to come looking for me they would be sent off track.

A post was put up on Rangers Media - which stayed up for some time without any of the site's moderators bothering to take it down - which suggested getting a van-load of boys together and driving up to Linwood to pay me a visit. It concluded:"We should show that bastard exactly what we think of him!"

I got sent a copy of it and put it up on Facebook. I wrote:"That's fine guys. If you want to thank me for my efforts then I'm 6ft 2in tall and totally bald. I'm usually standing by the John Greig statue outside Ibrox on match days handing out leaflets."

But the people who actually turned up at my house were the real deal. The people who talk big online are no danger to anybody. They live in a parallel universe. I termed them "Viagra keyboard users".Writing abusive messages and hiding behind false identities clearly made them feel hard.They pass themselves off as gangsters. The reality is they are usually pre-pubescent youths who sit in their bedrooms and post things to impress their halfwit pals.

But for every threat I received I got 30 messages thanking me for what I was doing. Some of the messages moved me to tears. Guys from as far afield as Australia and Hong Kong who felt helpless to do anything about the situation at the club contacted me. So did boys I went to school with and hadn't seen or spoken to for 30 years.

People would write:"We are so proud that it is one of our own who is doing this." Or they would say:"You are going to save Rangers." Unfortunately, I couldn't. I didn't have the money to do that.

I got to know lot of the people I have in the contacts on my phone, individuals I would call on a weekly basis when I was needing advice or help, through them sending me messages on Facebook. I am talking about lawyers, high-ranking police officers, those who work in senior positions in the civil service. I got to know them through social media.

I had people try to send me in the wrong direction with false information as well. But I got wise to that quite quickly.Whenever somebody contacted me anonymously I would endeavour to have somebody vouch for them and ascertain whether what they were telling me was genuine.

Sons of Struth are followed by a real cross section of society - from young lads who spend their days sitting in their houses, smoking dope and playing on their X Boxes to prominent QCs and well-known MPs.

The number of people who came to you with information was

amazing. They saw us as a vehicle for putting their message out if they had a grievance or were concerned about something which was being done behind the scenes. Quite quickly, we received a lot of information which we put out once we were able to verify it.

That became a task in itself. The vast majority of the stuff we were told we were unable to put out in the public domain. Not because we didn't believe it. It was just because we hadn't been able to stand it up. We had to be careful.

There were also times we were positive we were being fed misinformation in a deliberate attempt to discredit us. We have had to be wary of our sources. Much of my time was spent chasing up leads I received from emails, texts and social media.

A chap contacted me through Facebook one day and told me he wanted to show me something. We arranged to meet at Ibrox before a Rangers game one Saturday. He took out his mobile phone and he had a photograph on it of a bill from a city centre hotel for a room which a club director and a minor Glasgow media personality, both of whom I believed were married, had booked one night.

There was food, drink and the price of the accommodation on it. It came to a few hundred pounds. It was paid for using a Rangers Football Club credit card.

We could have taken it to the newspapers. But we decided not to. These things happen in all walks of life. Plus, the other person involved, who had done nothing to offend or upset me, may have had a husband. She was quite well-known. But I just wasn't comfortable acting on it. I didn't think it was my place to potentially break up a marriage. Were any children involved? I didn't know.

Everybody knew the director in question couldn't keep it in his trousers. Every fan was well aware of that. But I had heard worse stories about him than those regarding his marital infidelities. For me, there wasn't a story there. I actually thought the fact he had wasted the club's money was more of an issue. There were more negatives for somebody who was an innocent victim than positives for the Sons of Struth.

I was also shown a bill for several thousand pounds that was run up by club directors at a hotel coming back from an away game in Stranraer. Around 20 people were wined and dined by senior club officals.

Somebody inside the club had been quite happy to leak that Ally McCoist had taken the team to stay at Turnberry Hotel the night before a game. But they kept quiet about the hospitality they enjoyed on the return journey from a routine league game.

It seemed to me that the people in charge of the club thought they were so powerful they were indestructible. They were convinced they could do whatever the hell they liked. But when you really look at it some of the things they did were sheer lunacy. For a director of a club to blatantly pay for a room – which wasn't used overnight - on a club credit card was an arrogant and naive thing to do.

The individual responsible probably thought he was untouchable. But that is inevitably something that often happens to people in authority. They believe they are invincible and that becomes their downfall. I was quite happy to remind them they weren't. Whether it was from a distance or face to face.

The internet wasn't a place I frequented much before I started up Sons of Struth. I quickly found there are some people out there who are hard core. They are on it constantly. It becomes their entire life.

Once I started doing this people would come up to me when I was having a pint and say: "How are you doing Craig? I'm BillyBigGuns1690!" That is actually how they would introduce themselves. That is fine I suppose. But it's a bit peculiar when you really analyse it. It is hard to comprehend at times. I would ask them: "Oh, right! But what's your actual name?" They would reply: "It's Colin." The internet is just bananas.

CHAPTER 8

SHOW THE BOARD THE RED CARD

"I have had several emails from people who said they were led to believe the red card display was about apartheid so there seems to be come confusion among the fans."

David Somers, Rangers chairman.

THE first red card protest which we held at the League One game against Ayr United in the December of 2013 was a gamble. There are, you see, a surprising number of Rangers fans who go to Ibrox who really don't care what goes on at the club.

I had people stop me in street as I was handing out leaflets, look at me with puzzled expressions on their faces and say:"Doesn't Sir David Murray still own Rangers?"That is how out of touch some people were.They just wanted to go to a game on a Saturday, wave their flag, watch the team win or lose and then go back to their work on a Monday.They weren't 24/7 like me.

But word had filtered back to us after the previous protests that members of the board were putting it about that not all of the supporters had taken part and the unrest was nothing to be concerned about. So we felt we had to do something. But when we were discussing it I did say:"This could come back and kick us in the teeth."

The leaflet read:"Hold up this card in the 18th and 72nd minutes if you want this club cleansed of all links to Green, Ahmad and Whyte. If you are a shareholder make sure you are represented at the club AGM and vote. Use your voice at Ibrox, at the AGM and in the media to demand change."

We then listed 21 offences which we believed proved the board were unfit for purpose and should be replaced. They included blowing the £22 million raised at the IPO, trying to block The Requisitioners from holding a perfectly legitimate EGM and for awarding themselves huge bonuses for Rangers beating part-time teams to win the Third Division. It concluded: "It's an appalling record and we need to act now."

It was quite nerve-wracking beforehand. At the 15th minute my heart was thumping in my chest. In the 16th minute my stomach was tied in knots. It was horrible waiting to see if the protest you had helped to organise was going to be a success or not. But 10 seconds before the allocated time you can see folk getting their leaflets ready. Then you see them going up. It is only 10 or 20 seconds after it starts that you get to see the sort of impact it has had.

When you are sitting there having organised it you are, not to put too fine a point on it, shitting yourself. I can remember thinking: "Sons of Struth could be finished in a few seconds if nobody puts a card up." But when they did go up my reaction was: "Wow! We've done it again. They have bought into it. They feel the same as us." It made me so proud.

Before each protest we held brainstorming sessions. We had meetings of about a dozen or so fans, not always the same faces, at the Ivory Hotel and suggestions would get made. There would be representatives from the Union Bears, the Blue Order, the Rangers Supporters Trust, whoever. There would be guys there without any ties to any official organisation. Between us, we would always come up with something.

I can remember speaking to the newspaper journalist turned internet blogger David Leggat after one of the meetings. Leggo said: "Craig, when you told me your card idea I thought: 'That's never going to work!' But, by God, did it not just!" We always formulated a battle plan. But there was never any guarantee it would be a success. There was nothing to compare it to. We just hoped that we could pull it off.

When we first decided to protest in the 18th and 72nd minutes some folk said: "That'll never work! What if we get a goal?" But we agreed we couldn't protest before kick-off or at the end of the game. I personally wanted to do it for 10 minutes. I said: "We should do it from the 18th to the 28th minute." I was quickly slapped down and told: "No, Craig." Anyway, what we did worked a treat. I can't remember who came up with it. Everybody had an input in those get togethers.

I ended up coming up with the idea for the Union of Fans at one of those meetings. I was sitting there one day and I said: "Hold on a minute! You're from the trust, you're from the assembly, you're from the association, you're from the Blue Order. Guys, we have a 'Union of Fans' here." I thought it would be good to pay back the other organisations who had been involved in everything we had done whether it be manpower, ideas, whatever. We all dovetailed nicely. Everybody had contributed something. It also showed unity.

People used to ask me: "Who do you speak for?" I would say: "Sandy and me." Those were the only people we represented. Whenever we said anything a lot of people agreed with our stance. Although the Union of Fans only started being used the next year it was created in a meeting in a split second months before. It was all the same people saying the same things. We just packaged and presented in differently.

The only other group of any significance was The Vanguard Bears. We spoke to them and asked if they wanted us to come to the party. I don't think they disagreed totally with what we were doing. But they prefer to do their own thing. That was fine. I know a few guys who are involved in that organisation as a consequence of starting up the Sons of Struth. They have contacted me. But they can be quite clandestine and secretive. No disrespect to them, they are just into different things.

Going up behind the directors' box with a banner became a thing for me. My banner would change every couple of weeks. At one game it would say: "AGM NOW." The next week it would say: "SPIVS OUT." Whatever was topical really. The security staff became quite used to seeing me pop up at half-time and full-time. We would have a bit of banter.

The red card had bullet points on one side about who we were, what we were doing and why we were doing it. It also itemised some of the lies, around a dozen or so, that we had been told by the board. Getting so many leaflets printed cost between £800 and £1,200. Once again, the Ballieston True Blues came up with the money.

We didn't say anything that we couldn't back up in the leaflets. It felt so wrong that these guys were paying themselves huge bonuses for winning the league. Especially Brian Stockbridge. His bonus should have been based on the financial performance of the company. But he had a contract which stated he received a bonus because we won promotion. That wasn't a bonus it was a guarantee. Rangers were always going to win the Third Division. There was no danger they wouldn't.

Once the game kicked off I was obviously apprehensive. I had been running about the streets for a couple of hours making sure everybody handing out leaflets had a supply of them and they were being evenly distributed around the stadium. I was pretty busy. The last hour is absolute bedlam. I would have had to be an octopus to get them all handed out with the number of fans swarming towards me.

What was happening on the park just washed over you. You thought: "Is this going to work? Is this going to be the one that embarrasses us?" Then bang! It is an amazing feeling when you see all these people have bought into what we are trying to achieve. You feel vindicated.

I had to appreciate that the normal punter wasn't that involved. On a scale of one to ten in terms of involvement with Rangers I was at a ten. But some fans were just a five or a six. Others were a two. It made you worried.

As the clock got nearer and nearer, at 17:53, 17:54, 17:55, you got more apprehensive. A point was actually raised up by a boy at one of our meetings. He said: "Look, I don't mean to be pedantic, but do you know we're actually demonstrating in the 19th and 73rd minutes?" We all looked at him and said: "Oh do shut up!"

The attendance at the Ayr United game was 45,000. We printed 40,000 red leaflets. But we only managed to hand out around 30,000 before kick-off. So the most we could have got taking part in that protest was three quarters of the ground. But when you look at video footage and photographs of that day it looks like everybody who took a red card put it up. The visual message it sent out was quite impressive. It was phenomenal.

The statements by our chairman David Somers after the red card display were a disgrace. He claimed supporters thought it was an anti-apartheid demonstration and were confused. That is even though, as a schoolchild could tell you, that racist system of segregation had been abolished in South Africa nearly 20 years before.

He said: "I have had several emails from people who said they were led to believe the red card display was about apartheid so there seems to be come confusion among the fans."

He was basically accusing Rangers fans of being unable to read. One side of the leaflet was red, the other side had writing. That accusation coming from the chairman was disgusting and low. To try and spin it that way beggared belief. I don't know if he actually believed that or if it was blatant lies. Either way, he was off his head.

NAIVELY, I believed The Requisitioners could get in at the AGM. In the days leading up to it I felt it was going to be tight. I felt each side had around about 40 per cent of the vote. I thought the 20 per cent would have decided it. I thought the major investors had made their minds up and it was down to the wee guys to decide it. But I was probably still taking Laxey into account at that point.

Then I started hearing about votes they may have from this party and that investor. The day before the AGM I started getting phone calls from journalists. The board has been re-elected. The Requistioners have lost. How do you feel about it?

The postal votes were in and counted and the results were leaked to BBC Scotland. Al Lamont got the scoop on it. So actually going to the AGM was an anti-climax. It must be how a St. Mirren fan feels going to a cup final against Rangers. You know your team has lost before the game kicks off.

I got a phone call to go on Radio Scotland the night before the AGM and went down to appear on their sports show. It was the first time I had been in a radio studio. The presenter and the producer introduced themselves and told me what format the show was going to take. But I didn't know who was on the show.

When I went to take my seat Graham Spiers was sitting there

taking notes. I had been giving it to him tight on Twitter a couple of nights earlier. I thought: "This could get a bit awkward!" I knew he could be very anti-Rangers at times. He also had a lot more experience on live radio than I did. But to be fair to him he introduced himself and we had a chat.

Again, it was a strange experience. But it was enjoyable. We went for a coffee afterwards. A couple of days later he phoned me for an interview.

After the AGM my phone was red hot. I got a phone call from the BBC again asking me to go back in and do a follow-up piece. The producer said: "Look, because you were in last night and we want you to come in again tonight we will sort you out with some expenses."

I said: "No, you won't sort me out with any expenses. Because, one, you are the BBC and, two, that would mean I would put money in my own pocket." I declined the offer and always did so. Sometimes I wish I could have because of the financial predicament I ended up in.

That next night was even worse. It was Tom English. He had been pretty uncomplimentary about me a few days before. But he shook my hand and was absolutely fine. So I met two of the biggest perceived enemies of Rangers on consecutive evenings. Over the years I hadn't liked a lot of things they had written and said. But face-to-face they were both fine.

Fans had a go at me online for speaking to the BBC because Rangers had banned them. But if Sons of Struth had a campaign to have the players wear red and black socks we would get knocked for it. I didn't have an issue with it. When you are running a campaign and a national broadcaster offers you air time you would be stupid not to take it. It gets your message out to a larger audience. I was actually on the BBC live one day and told them I didn't like the BBC. I even appeared on Newsnight one evening after the announcement on the first tier tax tribunal appeal was made. But I thought the whole thing was a stitch up.

It was the first time I had been asked to go on a live television programme so I asked a lot of questions about it. I wanted to know who I would be on with. I was told it would just be a presenter interviewing me. It wasn't.

Angela Haggerty, who had edited a book called Downfall: How Rangers FC self-destructed written by an internet blogger who called himself Phil Mac Giolla Bhain and who was despised by Rangers supporters, was on as well. I asked what questions I was going to be asked. I was told and then asked different questions.

I had to go in to make-up before I went on screen to stop my baldy head dazzling the viewers. Then I was put in what they call The Green Room (thankfully, there was nothing green in it) and told I had to leave my mobile phone in there.

Unbeknown to me, Angela Haggerty had starting Tweeting that she was going on Newsnight Scotland with Craig Houston. So she knew beforehand who she was going on with. I, meanwhile, was told I would be asked certain questions by a presenter in a one-on-one interview. That, for me, wasn't right. It put the person on the other side of the debate at an advantage.

I was ushered through to the studio and didn't hear the presenter say Rangers had been stripped of titles. I didn't know until I got back later that night. A few people got in touch later telling me I should have challenged that. But I hadn't heard it.

The whole thing was peculiar. I had been in the BBC studios on a few occasions and had always been treated, even by people I disagreed with and had been publicly criticised by, guys like Tom English and Graham Spiers, well. I had never been made to feel unwelcome. They would always shake your hand and be pleasant to you. The journalists would always explain what would happen.

But as I was getting my make-up done before Newsnight the presenter Sarah Smith was sitting in the seat three feet away from me. When I started telling the girl doing my make-up what I was on for she didn't acknowledge me or introduce herself.

Even when we were both sat at the table waiting to do our interview, as a report by Richard Wilson on the appeal against the outcome of the first tier tax tribunal was being played, she didn't say a thing. I felt it was really odd. I thought: "This lady doesn't like me very much and I've never even spoken to her!"

Then out of the corner of my eye I saw what I took to be an autocue machine. Written on it, was " . . . and joining me now from

Westminster is Angela Haggerty ... ". I couldn't believe my eyes. I thought they must be interviewing her and then me. If I had known I was going to be on with anyone associated with Phil McThreenames I would have been ready.

That day I had watched the BBC documentary "The Men Who Sold The Jerseys" twice. It was meant to be investigative journalism. But I, and a lot of supporters, felt it pretty much concluded, before a verdict had been reached, that Rangers were guilty. I wanted to be clear in my own mind what they had said.

As soon as the debate started I thought: "This is a stitch up! I'm going to have a pop at the BBC here! I might not get asked back after this!" The first question was: "Can you really blame the demise of Rangers all on the taxman?" I said: "How it was portrayed in the media scared off investment. Documentaries done in this building suggest it was a done deal and Rangers owed £75 million."

I then decided, irrespective of what question was put to me, to ask her a question. I was going to say: "I know why I'm here, but could somebody explain why this lady, who is a Celtic supporter, is here?" But I didn't get the chance. I was cut off twice in mid-sentence. I was ushered straight off afterwards. Nobody thanked me for my time. It was a horrible experience.

I found out afterwards that Sarah Smith had been held at gunpoint by the Ulster Defence Association at their headquarters in West Belfast early in her career. It was suggested to me she had something against Rangers because of its associations with unionist and loyalist movements.

I was heavily slated after it. Many of the people who had a go were quite right too. But they didn't know the circumstances behind it.

I EXPECTED the board to get an odd boo at the AGM. But the level of aggression and hostility among the two or three thousand shareholders who attended took me aback. When the directors came onto the stage the place just erupted. To a man, everybody barracked them. There were chants of "sack the board". Several more unsavoury remarks were made. As they stood behind their seats waiting to take their places it continued. It probably only lasted for a few minutes. But it was constant. It seemed like an eternity.

Sandy and I were asked by lots of people in the build-up to the AGM what we were doing. We spoke about it and decided it was a business meeting and there are certain ways to conduct yourself in such a situation. Whether you liked the individuals involved or not was irrelevant. We decided to do nothing. Just turn up and cast a vote. It didn't require a great deal of discussion.

We even agreed that if there was any verbal abuse or jeering of the directors not to get involved. We would sit on our hands. That way Sons of Struth couldn't be blamed. We had already been falsely accused of being the perpetrators of unruly behaviour by the club. We genuinely did nothing. People claimed we planted people in the audience. That just did not happen.

Phil Maher, who works with one of the biggest institutional banks in the City of London, and George Letham, an extremely wealthy supporter, were two guys I had nothing to do with before the AGM. They probably asked the key questions. One was about Brian Sockbridge's bonus. The other was about the £6.5 million costs of the IPO. The shareholders went into meltdown at the answers they were given.

Phil asked about the costs of the IPO. Sitting behind the directors were four or five individuals, legal advisors and representatives of the nominated advisor, Daniel Stewart. One of them replied: "I'm not sure if we can answer that at an AGM." Phil said: "Aye you can, because I've just asked." The hands went over the microphone as they conferred for a few minutes. Then they decided they had to give a response.

So Brian Stockbridge started spouting all of these figures. They added up to more than £6.5 million. When he said ". . . and £2.5 million for financial advice . . . " I thought the shareholders were going to storm the stage and lynch him. I genuinely feared the guy wouldn't get out of the stadium in one piece. The backlash was ferocious. It was bedlam.

When he was asked how that was possible we received the stock answer again. "Because we were a business in trouble," he said. I thought the shareholders were going to storm the stage at that point. It was complete and utter tosh. The financial risk of the company wasn't an issue.

Graham Wallace, who had been appointed as chief executive the month before, spoke and many people were encouraged by how he conducted himself. But I wasn't especially optimistic myself. My gut instinct was:"This guy is just another face who will be dictated to".That changed to a degree later when I actually met him.

We came out of the AGM and hung around for a bit speaking to folk.As the crowd died away we went up to the Sherbrooke Castle Hotel in Pollokshields where The Requisitioners were doing a press conference. The usual suspects were there; Chris Graham, David Leggat, Mark Dingwall. It was like being at a wake.

Sandy got a call and said:"We have to go down to the Louden for a drink. Les, Michael, Clare and Gordon are there."They had been through the whole thing with us.

Gordon said:"Look, we want to show our appreciation for what you have done."

I said:"What I've done? You're the ones who helped me."

They presented me with two crystal glasses with the Sons of Struth logo on it. I nearly broke down. I was very emotional.

Sandy and I went back up to the Sherbrooke. The media conference was still going on so we went to the bar. Andy McLintock, a stockbroker who worked in London who I had got to know, was sitting with one of the institutional investors I had met for an Indian the night before.

This guy controlled about eight per cent of the club. The four of us sat down. After a while I burst out laughing. Andy said: "What's up?" I said:"Look at this table.What other circumstances in the world would bring us together? We have me, a loudmouth anti-board fan, you a professional stockbroker, one of the main investors in the club and an ex-football hooligan who spent time in jail for dealing ecstasy tablets."

I got to learn from dealing with institutional investors that they don't like change.They want to put their money in and then take it out five or 10 years later. If they win 51 per cent of the time they make millions of pounds. The fan thinks: "They have £1 million invested in Rangers!" But that could be 0.05 per cent of their whole investment portfolio that year. If the club goes to the wall and they lose every penny it is not that disastrous for them.

It is possible the likes of Ahmed and Green knew that and had worked the system before. Once they have talked them into buying in they are left alone to get on with the project. We are emotionally attached to the club. These guys are financially attached to the club. But in the grand scheme of things it genuinely doesn't matter to them. They don't vote for change at AGMs 99.9 per cent of the time. They just do a postal vote and tick a box to keep the same guys in. It would take something really frightening to make them act.

I would have loved to have been proved wrong. I would have loved whoever was in charge of Rangers to be shown to be capable and good and professional and trustworthy. I would have loved them to be transparent and honest. I would have loved them to stop telling lies about fans. But I doubted it would happen.

I will be a Rangers fans until the day they put me in a box. So I knew we would win one day. I knew none of them would be there for that length of time. It was just a matter of when we would win and how much damage had been done to the club by then.

If The Requisitioners had won that AGM Sons of Struth would still have been on the go trying to achieve our three aims. But the folk in charge would have been easier to deal with. So the battle would never have been over that day.

CHAPTER 9

SANDY EASDALE'S HAIR

"I'm scared to go for a haircut."

Sandy Easdale, Rangers football board chairman.

MY first contact with Sandy Easdale's lawyers came after the AGM. I think the Rangers board members must have thought that after they had clung on to power we would disappear and everything would settle down and return to normal. But as the song says: "The cry was No Surrender!" We took Christmas off and then started again.

I needed some time off to get my head together anyway. The relationship I had been in for three years was breaking down. I wouldn't say it was entirely down to Sons of Struth. Cracks had started to appear before that got up and running. But it definitely didn't help. Plus, my business was beginning to be adversely affected. I was working all the time on other things.

After the AGM my girlfriend Tracy sat me down and said: "The amount of time and effort you're putting into this is taking over your life." She made me aware that she felt she was second best to Sons of Struth. I'm not sure if that was true, but I could understand how she felt and why she had started to think that way.

She said: "Could we just have this Sunday with your phone switched off and no Sons of Struth. We'll go for a walk up the River Gryffe, get lunch at a pub and a have couple of glasses of wine."

But that Sunday my phone went at eight o'clock in the morning and it didn't stop all day. It was Rangers fans, it was journalists, it was people involved in some way with the whole process. She was right and I was wrong. I let it take over my life. Nobody made me do it. I started something with my pal Sandy Chugg. We didn't think it would get so big and time-consuming. I let it happen. But I was so invested in it I couldn't stop.

Tracy, too, thought the AGM would be an end to it. She thought she would get her Craig back after it. If we had won that might have been the case. We still would have kept an eye on things and ensured Ibrox was secure, we had a board we could be proud of and the club produced a set of clean accounts. But, of course, the board survived.

It was a tight Christmas because money was so short. Santa Claus still came to visit my kids. But it wasn't a nice time. My personal finances were in such a state. Somehow, we managed to scrape together enough cash to book a cheap holiday in January.

But that was when I started to get the first emails from Peter Watson, the lawyer at Levy Macrae who acted for Sandy Easdale. He was unhappy with adjectives used to describe James and Sandy Easdale on the Sons of Struth Facebook page. They were being likened to two notorious brothers who came from the East End of London in the 1960s. Not by me, I should say. By other people.

I got an email on a Monday outlining things which they were unhappy with that had been put on my Facebook page. It read: "Take it down or we will sue you." They were worded very heavily.

Then on the Wednesday my mother phoned me. She said: "There's a lawyer's letter here for you." When my marriage was breaking down some years before that, I moved back in with my parents for a few weeks. So when she told me that, I just assumed it was something to do with my separation. I told my mum: "I'll pick it up on Sunday when I come over to see you with the kids". But when I opened it up it turned out to be an exact copy of the email I had received.

It basically said: "Take this down or we will take you to the Court of Session." It was bizarre. I thought: "Surely that is the third or fourth letter you send?" It was very heavy-handed. Being naive about how these things work I thought it was serious. After a while, if I got a lawyer's letter or if a sheriff officer turned up at the door, I didn't get that uptight about it. But back then it was different.

The letters started coming in thick and fast. I would get one on a Monday and then get another one on the Wednesday. Sandy and I talked about it and decided to close the Facebook page. The legal threats and lawyer's letters had become an almost daily occurrence. It was never anything that I had written. Sandy Chugg didn't go on the page. I was going on holiday and wouldn't be able to monitor it. So I shut it down.

When the first letter came to my mother's house I got straight back to Peter Watson. I emailed him. I wrote: "How did you get my mother's address?" Unbeknown to me at the time, there is something called legal professional privilege. That basically means a lawyer can go and get your address by whatever means he wants. He doesn't have to tell you how he obtained it.

But I didn't need him to tell me. I knew he had got it from Rangers. When I had left home and got married I was hopeless at returning my season book renewal form, ticking the boxes for the games that I wanted and generally dealing with all of the paperwork involved in that. My father got fed up with me and eventually said he would deal with it. So all the correspondence between Rangers and me went to my parent's flat in Kinning Park where they had moved to by that time.

So I contacted Rangers to complain and in February I was invited up to Ibrox meet with Graham Wallace. I sat in his office for two and a half hours. Only five minutes of that meeting was taken up with discussion about the data protection issue that I had. He said to me: "Look Craig, I've investigated this and we've definitely not given your address out." I said: "But I've never lived at that address." His face went a different colour.

But I told him: "Listen, I'm glad you've told me you're not at fault. I'm not stupid. I know some lassie in the ticket office has been asked for that address by somebody far higher up the food chain and has given it out. I'm quite happy with what you're telling me. But you know and I know what's happened here."

I was still concerned. At that point in time, Sandy Eadale and his lawyer were saying: "You're responsible for what everybody else is writing on your Facebook page." Their case was that I was liable for it. Every time I received a communication I reacted to it. I removed the offensive post and put up an apology.

When news of what was happening came out, I started getting contacted by all sorts of lawyers and even QCs who were supportive of Sons of Struth. They told me they would look at it. I forwarded emails to several people in the legal profession and received guidance. They were all, to a man, of the opinion that I wouldn't get sued because it wouldn't stand it up in court.

It was well known that Sandy Easdale had been convicted of VAT fraud and had served time at Her Majesty's pleasure. Somebody was making comments about that. His lawyers were of the view that wasn't allowed because of the time which had elapsed since the charge. To them, it was a spent conviction.

I would sometimes question that. They would reply quoting lengthy legal passages. So I would just delete it and put up an apology. That seemed to me to be fair and sensible. I was moderating the page properly and monitoring it regularly.

Then a strange thing happened. I had a 45 minute telephone conversation after the AGM with Jack Irvine. He was probably one of the most notorious characters in this whole saga. There were many reasons for that. But one of the main ones was that he was exposed for sending an email making derogatory comments about John Greig after the man who was voted Greatest Ever Ranger stood down from the board during Craig Whyte's reign.

Jack had started sending me emails before the AGM. It was comical. He would have a dig at me. I would have a pop back at him. It was nothing more than that. After the board held onto power he sent me an email saying that I should just retire gracefully and accept defeat. I thought: "Bollocks to that!"

When we started up again his reaction was to phone me up and tell me how great Ally McCoist was, how he was great pals with our manager, how the board were good guys, how we had got it wrong, how Paul Murray and Malcolm Murray weren't the best for Rangers.

When you are dealing with somebody who is talking like that, when you know that what is coming out of their mouth is total garbage, you don't even listen. As he was speaking to me, I was thinking: "He's knows he's talking rubbish! I know he's talking rubbish. But if I confront him it's just going to turn into an argument." So I didn't even bother.

Towards the end of the conversation he said to me: "Tell your pals, Chris Graham, Mark Dingwall, David Leggat, anybody who does stuff online, to watch their backs, because one of you is going to lose your car, your house, your savings, your business, the lot." That was quite a harsh warning. I said: "Aye, nae bother Jack, bye."

But within weeks the letters started. I subsequently learned that Jack Irvine and Peter Watson were very close friends. Some people would even suggest they were in business together. It was of no real surprise that the two things were hand in hand. If you piss off Jack Irvine then Peter Watson comes after you. I am sure that in their own minds they are like Batman and Robin.

If somebody asks me to do something in a civil manner there is a fair chance I will do it. If somebody tells me to do something there is a fair chance I will tell them to go and take a running jump to themselves. So a lawyer and a PR man who represented people I didn't like telling me to do this and do that had absolutely no chance.

I was made aware from somebody inside Ibrox that Jack Irvine's company Media House was going to lose its contract with Rangers. But I wasn't sure if that was the case so I didn't tell a soul. Not even my co-founder.

When it did come to fruition in March, I came to think I had been told because they knew how much I had been battered. There was no hidden agenda. I think I was told because I was wronged over a few of the issues involved. It was wrong that a supporter was being persecuted by a company employed by the club.

When the news came out that Media House had lost the Rangers contract I sent Jack Irvine an email. It said: "Sorry to hear about you losing your job. Remember what you told me? Accept defeat graciously and move on. Well, you should do that." I haven't heard from him since.

I must have had a dozen or so letters between the first one and the one that threatened to sue me. I became friendly through Facebook with a lady whose husband was a lawyer. They sat in the same section as me at Ibrox. So I arranged to meet him at half-time during a game to show him some of the correspondence I had received to get his professional opinion.

As I was going into Ibrox that day I got an email from Peter Watson. He was asking for my postal address. My reply to him was: "Well, we've nothing outstanding. Everything you have complained about before has been dealt with. Plus, because we have been conducting our business electronically I see no reason to furnish you with my home address."

At half-time I met the lawyer and showed him the email requesting my address. That was when I saw I had another email from Peter Watson. It said: "Fine. If you don't want to give me your postal address I'll instruct sheriff officers to go to the only address we have for you to obtain your current address."

The message basically was: "Tell me where you live or I'll send sheriff officers round to your 70-year-old parents' house." I was disgusted and very upset. The lawyer I spoke to said: "That's terrible. That's not right."

As the second half kicked off I showed the message to my dad. He was appalled too. He started telling his friends around about him in the stand. All these old boys couldn't believe what they were hearing and started mouthing off about it. I got angrier and angrier as the game went on. Five minutes before kick-off I walked over to the directors' box.

When I got there one of the security guards, who I was on first name terms with, came over and said: "How are you doing Craig?"

I replied: "Any chance you could get Graham Wallace to come and have a word with me?"

He asked: "Why?"

"Because that bastard Easdale is threatening to send sheriff officers to my parents' house. It's ridiculous. Somebody has to stop them. Somebody has to tell them: 'Enough is enough'."

A few minutes later the chief executive's secretary, who I had met a few times by this stage, came up to speak to me. She said: "Craig, this isn't the time or the place. Give us a call tomorrow and I'll set up a meeting." I was happy with that.

But just then the directors started leaving their seats and Sandy Easdale walked over. He said: "Do you want to talk to me?" To be fair to the man, he would always stop and speak. From that point on he never once ignored me. I might not have believed what he had to say when he did mind.

He said: "What's up?"

"What's up? This is getting personal now. I've just got an email from your lawyer telling me he is sending sheriff officers to my parents' door to get my address. That's over the line Sandy!"

"Well, you get personal with me."

"Hang on a minute, every letter I've received from your lawyer is about what somebody else has said. Explain to me how I have got personal with you."

What he said next became an online sensation.

"You're that personal that even when you're apologising you take the piss out of me. You even slag off my hair! I'm scared to go for a haircut because people will think I'm doing it because you've ridiculed me."

The first few minutes of our conversation were quite heated. It calmed down as the stadium emptied. And I did laugh at that remark about his hair.

He said: "What do you want me to do?"

"I want you to get something from your lawyer telling me you're not sending sheriff officers to my parents' door. Because if you don't I can quite easily get a newspaper photographer up to take a picture of them with your letter looking awful worried. That'll not be a nice photograph for you. Do you want me to do that?"

"Well obviously I don't."

"Well, get something to me by noon tomorrow or I'll go to the papers."

I shook his hand and left the ground.

I got a phone call from Keith Jackson at the Daily Record the next morning. He asked me: "What happened to you last night at Ibrox?" I said: "How do you know?" He said: "The photos are all over the internet!" Fans had taken photographs of us speaking on their mobile phones and had put them on the internet. The Record ran a photo of me with my finger in Sandy Easdale's face.

I was expecting Sandy Easdale to get on the phone to his lawyer, tell him to calm down and email me. What I got was the complete opposite. I received a Court of Session summons for £200,000 for defamation of character. I needed a new pair of boxer shorts after opening that letter. I looked at it and said: "That's an awful lot of zeroes." I must admit I froze and then went into a blind panic for a while.

There was a list of six or seven comments which other people had made on Facebook. I was also offered a gagging order. If I signed it the action would be dropped. But it stipulated I wouldn't be able to mention the name Sandy Easdale. It was so unworkable. I would have needed to shut down the page.

When I got back home the night before I had received numerous messages from people on Facebook who had heard I had spoken to him asking me what had happened. I was hopeful the whole thing would be done and dusted the next day so I said nothing. I was quite vague. I just said: "I was speaking to him about an email I had received from his lawyer." I left it at that. I didn't want to tell anybody I was getting sued because I thought it might affect my chances of reaching an agreement.

But when I received the summons and the gagging order I decided to tell all of the Rangers supporters who had been asking me what had happened during the conversation. I kept the fact I was being sued secret. For some reason, people really picked up on the line about him being afraid to go and get a haircut. By that stage, nobody had really been slagging off his hair. But one day, in a throwaway remark that I didn't think twice about, I wrote: "He's even got stupid hair!"

I burst out laughing when he told me. I said: "C'mon Sandy we're all big boys!" To be fair to him, he laughed too. That was the strange thing with him. You could have a bit of banter. It was bizarre. We would never be buddies. But there was a certain amount of humour in our relationship.

Within 20 minutes somebody had set up a Twitter account called Sandy Easdale's Hair. The internet went into meltdown. People made up fake Sandy Easdale hair care products. There were pictures of Lego men with Sandy Easdale haircuts. A photograph of Sandy Easdale with Keith Lemon's wig superimposed onto it appeared. Fans started calling the directors "The Wigs" after that.

It was like that for the next two weeks. None of it was vicious or unpleasant. It was comedy gold. Some of the people who are online are very humorous. I have been the subject of some of it. I have had pictures of Uncle Fester from The Munsters with a Sons of Struth badge on his shirt. You just had to laugh at it.

This all happened at the end of February and the beginning of March. It was two months after the AGM. It didn't help my relationship with Tracy at all. She thought a line in the sand had been drawn. Next thing she knows I am getting sued for £200,000. She was devastated. She thought she was going to lose her house.

Despite my unease at what they were trying to do, I seriously toyed with the idea of signing the gagging order. It was as much pressure as I had been under at any stage in my life. It was horrible. It doesn't matter if somebody said: "You'll be alright. There's nothing to worry about." Until I sat down in a room with a lawyer to go over it I was living with the possibility I could lose everything.

The court summons took over my life. It consumed me all day every day. I spoke to people about it. I got legal advice. It was constant. I would sometimes go to my bed at night and not be able to get to sleep. I would lie awake thinking: "Will I just sign that gagging order? If I shut down the Facebook page my life can go back to normal. I could start spending more time with my girlfriend and my kids".

I was hardly seeing my son by this stage. He was highly embarrassed. He was at the Stenhousemuir game in September when we had our first protest. The next game he went to was the Ramsdens Cup final against Raith Rovers the following April. He got stopped by a teacher in his school one day and asked: "Is that your dad who's getting sued by Sandy Easdale?" That is an uncomfortable thing for a teenager to deal with. Before too long, when we were meant to be seeing each other he would, more often than not, have things to do with his pals.

I was never told: "Ben doesn't want to see you because he's embarrassed you're the Sons of Struth guy." But I certainly saw a lot less of him. And he didn't want to go to football with me. So it was very tempting to sign the bit of paper, bin the Facebook page and wind up Sons of Struth. I could see my kids more, go to matches as a normal person and save my business.

I started to get suspicious I was being followed around that time.

I would catch something in my rear view mirror as I was driving that would make me jump. I would see somebody loitering near my parked car acting strangely. I just put it down to paranoia and dismissed it. I was going through a stressful time. But one specific incident couldn't have been anything but me being tailed.

I had been contacted by somebody about my dealings with Peter Watson and the legal threats I was receiving from Sandy Easdale. He was just a Rangers fan who was unhappy with what was happening to me. But he had information which he felt would be useful to me.

He wanted to speak to me because he knew what was going on was being done just to shut me up. He didn't want to meet me in a public place or in my house so we agreed to sit in my car and talk. I arranged to meet him on Paisley Road West. I arrived five minutes early, parked my car and nipped into a nearby shop to buy some cigarettes.

When I came out of the shop I stood and had a smoke. There was a guy wearing a shirt and tie sitting in a silver Volvo parked two cars behind me. There were no offices in the vicinity where somebody dressed like that may have worked so he stuck out. I thought: "Why is he sitting there?" He wasn't having his lunch. He was just sitting doing nothing.

I had taken advice from people who were knowledgeable about what I should do in that sort of situation. I had spoken to current and former police officers and to senior army personnel. I wasn't wandering around looking over my shoulder 24 hours a day seven days a week or anything like that. But I was wary. I thought that situation was a bit odd.

The man I was due to meet arrived and I signalled to him to go down a side street. I told him: "I didn't want to meet you there. There was somebody sitting out there who was unnerving me."

On another occasion, I had arranged to meet someone who I had voiced my concerns about having my mobile phone hacked to in the city centre. We had agreed that, rather than set a time and date for our rendezvous days in advance and alert whoever may have been monitoring my conversations, he would phone me at home before he wanted to see me and then we would get together at an agreed location five or 10 minutes after that.

The upshot of that was I ran out of the house without a penny. I was driving along in the left hand lane waiting to go across the Albert Bridge and I realised I had no money for the parking meter and would have to go back to the flat to get my wallet. So I crossed four lanes and turned right in order to do that.

As I looked in my mirror before I turned I saw the same silver Volvo a few cars behind me. As I turned it did exactly the same. It crossed all four lanes to go right. The driver waited until I was nearly out of sight. But I managed to spot what he had done.

I immediately thought back to the advice I had been given. I had been told to double back on myself on a few occasions if I was in that scenario. It was also suggested that before I pulled into a cul-de-sac or dead end, as the street outside my flat was, I should pull in on a main road for a while and left the traffic behind pass me.

I was in the Tradeston area of the city by that stage and it was easy to double back on myself a few times as there is a one way system in place. After that I stopped on Paisley Road West and waited for a few minutes. I eventually got my money and headed into the city centre.

The person I was meeting was in Buchanan Street. I parked into West Campbell Street, got out of my car and lit up a cigarette. Lo and behold, the same silver Volvo drove past. It could be coincidence. But I don't believe that. I had seen the same car in three different locations in a short space of time. I firmly believe I was being followed. There were other incidences similar, but not as striking, to that as well.

Billy Montgomery took me to see the lawyer who was best qualified in Glasgow to deal with the kind of legal issue I was facing. The chap was a Rangers supporter. To this day I don't know if he did it free of charge or if somebody paid for it. They sat with me for a couple of hours and the lawyer went through everything.

He was convinced the Court of Session would have thrown it out. What normally happens when you draw up a summons is that somebody takes it to the court, a sheriff signs it and then it is handed to the person being sued. But the sheriff doesn't need to sign it. They can say: "That's a lot of nonsense!" The summons I had didn't have a signature of a sheriff. The lawyer said: "That's a dead giveaway it is not going anywhere."

Andy Smillie, a diehard Rangers fan who runs his own successful scaffolding company, had been on the phone to me regularly throughout the whole saga offering his support and he knew I was going to see this lawyer. He phoned me a couple of hours after the meeting. He had been told what had happened. He asked me: "What are you going to do now?" I said: "I'm happy to take one for the team on this. I'll go to court."

I was always of the opinion that if the matter went to court then, win or lose the case, they would have lost. The fans had turned on them as it was. If there had been a full-blown court case it would have been very badly received.

Andy said to me: "Craig, I didn't want to tell you this before in case it influenced your decision, but now you've decided to do it I'll let you know. The next time you get a letter from that man's lawyer just send them back a two word message. Fuck. Off. Then phone me and I'll arrange a top lawyer to defend you and I'll pay the bill."

I have since been told by others that Andy was prepared to pay my £200,000 fine if I was found guilty in court.

He was in a meeting with Sandy Easdale some time after that about another matter and my name came up in conversation. Andy said: "You don't get it do you? See that boy you were trying to sue? Do you know I was paying his legal fees?" Apparently, Sandy went an awfully funny colour.

Andy continued: "I'll tell you something else. I would've paid his £200,000 if you had won the case. That was ridiculous what you tried to do to that boy."

I was reassured by legal advice which told me I would be fine. But, deep down, I still thought: "How dare they! I must be the only football fan in Britain to be sued by a director." They kept dressing it up and saying: "This isn't Rangers." Which it wasn't. But that didn't wash with me. Somebody at the club should have got a hold of Sandy Easdale and said: "You don't do that."

Derek Johnstone had even gone on Radio Clyde one night and

said Sandy Easdale was within his rights to sue me. That made me feel terrible. He had been a hero of mine growing up. It was horrible.

We had a protest after the story was made public. I nearly started crying inside Ibrox. Because in the 72nd minute the whole crowd, almost to a man, started shouting: "Easdale! Easdale! Get to fuck!" There had been the odd anti-Easdale chant here and there before that but nothing on the same level.

I knew that was because he was suing me. It was the fans showing solidarity with a fellow supporter. Some of them wouldn't have known my name. To this day, some of them still won't have heard of me. But many will have heard that Sandy Easdale was suing a Rangers fans. My dad was sitting next to me that day. He said: "That's because of you." As I say, I nearly broke down.

CHAPTER 10

BILL STRUTH'S BOWLER HAT

"You're a captive audience."

Dave King, Rangers supporter.

THE pressure I felt under when I was being sued for £200,000 by Sandy Easdale was immense. I was on edge constantly as a result.

In the first 12 months that Sons of Struth was on the go I was probably averaging four hours sleep a night. I would lie awake for hours digesting what had happened that day in the news - because the stories about Rangers at that time were pretty much constant - and thinking about my next move.

The worst time was in the run-up to the AGM. I would go over things in my mind again and again and again. I would say to myself: "What haven't I covered? What haven't I done? What more can I do? Can I send more emails? Can I organise more protests?"

I started to think I was personally responsible for every single person who had held up red cards at our protests. I genuinely believed I would have let down the thousands of people who had looked to us for guidance and had backed us. I would experience visions of the faces of all of the people who had come to meetings, distributed leaflets and helped us throughout the process. It was a horrible time.

Sandy Chugg saw it and became concerned. I had suffered from depression on and off in the past. It had first happened when I was working down in London for a spell. I was commuting between there and Glasgow at weekends. That was a difficult situation and was probably one of the factors which contributed to the break-up of my marriage. I went through a bout of depression without realising it. It was only when I came out the other side of it that it dawned on me what it had actually been.

Depression is a terrible, horrible, savage thing. You get to a point where you are convinced there is no way out of the predicament you are in. I would compare it to being stuck at the bottom of the well and reaching for the sky but being unable to scale the walls. I actually started to think:"Would the world be a better place without me?" It got so bad at one point that I even considered ways I could end my life. It didn't seem abnormal to think that way either.

I was in a well-paid job at the time. Money wasn't an issue. My business partner and I had two company cars at the time. One was a Bentley and the other one was a Jaguar. But the pressures of work, of being away from home, of not being around to help raise my young children, all took a toll.

Managing my own business was a large part of it. I was in charge of a company which was generating millions of pounds a year in revenue and had several staff members. There were great expectations of me. I got to a point where my head couldn't cope. I started thinking crazy thoughts which, to me at the time, seemed completely rational.

I had even gone so far as to contemplate crashing my car as I was driving back to Glasgow on the M6 and killing myself. That seemed rational to me in the appalling condition I was in. I would think:"If I don't drive up the road with six cans of Red Bull and the air conditioning on full blast this Friday as usual I'll get really tired and it'll be easier to crash my car."

To a normal person, that seems utterly insane. But you get so down that is how you can think. You don't think:"Jesus Christ! I'm thinking about doing myself in here!" It is like having a heavy rucksack on your back weighing you down.

Thankfully, I came out of that situation after getting a fright on the road home when the wheels of my car started to hit the rumble strip. It was only then that I realised I must be depressed. The next time it occurred, when my marriage finally broke down, I could see it coming and I sought help. I made an appointment to see a doctor.

Even before I went to the chemist with a prescription the dark cloud that was hanging over me was lifted. Just speaking to somebody about it was like taking a drug in itself. You don't speak to people about these things. At least, men in Scotland don't. You don't share your feelings when you are depressed. But just getting it off your chest is a help.

The doctor asked me about my sleeping, about my diet and various other things. Then he told me: "You're clinically depressed." It was almost a relief. You can differentiate between depression and reality and you can do something about it. Once you accept you're unwell you can take affirmative action.

I could see the same signs in the run-up to the AGM. Instead of a number of things in my life taking up my energy, focus and time, just one thing dominated my every waking hour. It became all-consuming. I started to think I couldn't cope. I was getting panic attacks. I was waking up after being asleep for an hour or two covered from head to toe in sweat.

When I was getting sued I hit another real low. I started to think: "I can't cope with this. I'm never going to get out of this." I realised how much this whole campaign had impacted on my life. I don't own much, but I could have lost everything. Just because I had stood and voiced my disquiet about how my football club was being run.

I also started to think of my personal life. My relationship with my girlfriend had ended because Sons of Struth had become my life. That started to really sink in at that point. But by then it was too late. I had also gone weeks without access to my son and daughter. I genuinely believed that those relationships, the most important in my life, were in jeopardy.

My son was a teenager and, like most teenagers, he was embarrassed by his da'. When his old man was plastered across the front and back pages of the newspapers every other day and was popping up on television and the radio I'm quite sure he didn't think: "Good on you pops for standing up for the Rangers!"

I don't think he got ridiculed for it. Most of his pals are Rangers supporters and I'm sure they must have thought it was quite cool that I was giving it tight to the board. But he decided he wanted to stop coming to see his dad on a Sunday and stop going to the football with him. His mum was concerned too. She thought we were going to games and ripping up stadiums. I am sure she put pressure on him as well.

Going to Rangers games with my son was always a nice experience for me. I lost that for a long time. For a long time after Sons of Struth started I didn't go to one match with him. If my son didn't want to come and see me then my daughter wouldn't come either.

When all that happens and you are feeling down you do ask yourself if it is all worth it. Your relationship is breaking up. Your business is suffering. You aren't seeing your children. I definitely fell down to the bottom of that well again. It was hard to see a way out at times.

There were occasions when I would storm out of the house after an argument. I would find myself sitting alone in a car park somewhere. I would see a tree and crazy thoughts would enter my head. Then I would snap out of it.

I had a few people who really pulled me through that. Billy Montgomery was constantly on the phone. Sometimes every hour. It wasn't all about Rangers either. Big Boris was a rock too. I christened them my "verbal Valium". They really kept me going. They didn't know it at the time, but they may very well have saved my life.

I had been on anti-depressant medication on and off for years. I phoned up and got a prescription for it. Whether the tablet works or not almost becomes irrelevant. Just walking to the chemist and feeling that you are doing something to deal with the situation is therapeutic in itself. You believe life is going to get better.

I also bought self-help books and taught myself relaxation methods. When you work in sales there is a lot of emphasis placed on getting yourself in the right frame of mind. As a sales manager your job is to make sure the people working under you have their heads right. There is a lot you can take out of that when you are depressed and down low. I benefited from that around that time.

Sandy Chugg was fantastic too. He had seen what was happening and would say to me: "Craig, you're suffering here." He was a real friend. But it was a horrible time. Every minute of every hour of every day I had a £200,000 law suit hanging over me. That lasted about a month.

There was no time limit on the gagging order. It was open ended. I could sign it any time. But once I had received the legal advice I decided to ignore it.

There were some light-hearted moments to ease the tension. I went to the Scottish Cup replay with Albion Rovers at New Douglas Park in Hamilton while this was going on. As I went up to take my seat in the main stand next to my pals, who knew what I was going through, I could see them killing themselves laughing.

Andy Smillie stopped me and gave me his normal warm greeting. He said: "Have you seen who you've got for company tonight?" I looked up and two rows away from where I was going to be sitting were the Rangers directors – including James and Sandy Easdale. I walked past, gave them a nod and said: "Evening gents! No need to worry about me tonight. I'm only here to see the Rangers."

WHEN the story finally went in the paper the internet went into meltdown. Even people who didn't like Sons of Struth, didn't like me personally, didn't even support Rangers in some cases, were appalled. I even had some Celtic fans sending me nice messages. You normally only see support like that being extended across the Old Firm divide if a great player, the likes of a Jim Baxter, a Sandy Jardine or a Jimmy Johnstone, has died.

People were outraged. There were calls to radio phone-ins about it. Huge threads on online message boards debated it. Chants started at matches. The story just exploded. I think the pressure turned onto Sandy Easdale at that point. He tried to spin it like it was a personal thing and nothing to do with the club. But that didn't wash with folk.

I soon heard that the Rangers Fans Fighting Fund had held talks about financing my defence. The fund was set up to help after the club went into administration in 2012 and most of the fans had contributed to it. But I hadn't been involved with it in any way.

I felt uneasy about it. I didn't feel it was right. My personal opinion was that most people, myself included, had donated to that fund on the understanding the money would be used to protect Rangers.

But some people felt that as a fan, I was Rangers and that is why some members of the fund board felt it would be a good idea to use that money to help me. They had a meeting and the sole purpose of it was to discuss using a portion of the money to help a fellow Bear who was in trouble. The next step was to ballot the supporters on it. But things didn't get that far.

Jim Hannah, the supporters' liaison officer at Rangers, is on the board of the fighting fund. So the club would have become aware of what was being discussed through him. I got a phone call from Jim one day. He said: "I think it would be a good idea if you and Sandy Easdale both came in to Ibrox, sat in an office and had a private and confidential conversation." I think they were desperate to get the matter settled before the fighting fund ruled on it.

A time and date was agreed for the meeting. Beforehand, it was agreed that we would both sign non-disclosure documents about the meeting. I did that when I got to the stadium. But within hours of the meeting I received a phone call from a reporter at The Sun newspaper asking me to comment.

I said: "I can't comment on it. Legally, I'm not allowed to talk about it."

The Sun journalist said: "Well, Sandy Easdale was quite happy to talk about the meeting."

I thought: "What was the point in signing the non-disclosure document?"

I am unable to talk about what was said or what went on in that meeting because of that agreement. But I can say that it was nothing short of outrageous. My blood was boiling at certain points during it. The hairs on the back of my arms were standing up at times. I thought: "I am sitting here in one of the most historic rooms in one of the most historic stadiums in Scotland - listening to this!"

We were making polite chit chat before the meeting and I told him I was hoping to take my son to the Ramsdens Cup final. Now, if you are a supporter of a club, playing in a cup final is quite important. You would think it would be the same for somebody who sat in the directors' box. But his response left me speechless. He said: "The Ramsdens Cup final? Is that the game we have to play in Edinburgh?" That suggested to me he was neither a big Rangers man nor a particularly switched-on club official.

I sat in the manager's office with Sandy Easdale for two hours. First of all, that wasn't a working room as far as I was concerned. It is more like a museum. Like most other Rangers fans I have gone on guided tours of Ibrox. But it was the only room in the main stand I hadn't been in. It should have been a thrill to sit in there for so long. But I was surprised and actually quite disgusted we were in there.

I was surrounded by important artefacts from the club's history. It has the actual ink well that Bill Struth used to write letters with. The walls were covered with photos of John Greig, Jock Wallace, Walter Smith, men who were Rangers through and through. I was there with somebody who didn't appear to know where Rangers were playing a cup final.

It got worse and worse. After the meeting had finished, I said to Sandy: "What's that hat on the coat stand?"

He said: "You'll love that. That's Bill Struth's bowler hat."

I went over to have a closer inspection. I was a little in awe of it. I was peering at it like you would look at a museum exhibit, with my hands behind my back. It was pristine on the outside. It was only when you peeked inside it that you could see it was slightly faded and worn.

I was dumbstruck that I was just inches away from the very bowler hat that Bill Stuth had worn one day. At this point Sandy jumped up, lifted the hat off the coat stand, stuck it on my head and started dancing around me singing: "You're not the real Bill Struth! Your head's too big!"

I screamed: "Sandy! Get that hat off my fucking head and put it back where it belongs!"

It's a peculiar piece or my club's history. But it is fascinating as well. I was horrified that somebody should treat it with so little respect.

I walked out of that office feeling physically sick. Some of the comments made were shocking, some of the terminology used was appalling. The conversation was akin to me sitting with some of my mates in a pub in Glasgow. I kept having to remind myself: "This man sits in the directors' box at Rangers on match days? The John Patons, John Lawrences, David Holmeses and the Lawrence Marlboroughs wouldn't, I am sure of it, have acted or spoken in such a manner. You hear tales of these men mucking in and helping out at turnstiles. Then you see what we have today."

But Sandy Easdale probably wouldn't have known who John Paton, John Lawrence, David Holmes and Lawrence Marlborough were. When you heard rumours about how the people who were running Rangers behaved it was one thing. But when it was in front of your eyes in a place that you regard to be sacred it was a real shock. When he showed no respect for the history and traditions of our football club it took me aback.

I was in the driving seat when it came to our stand-off. If I had asked Sandy Easdale to give me £10,000 at that point I would have got it. I am quite sure about that. He was in a no-win situation. I told him both before and after the meeting to drop the case. But what he wanted was to come out of it all without losing face. He wanted to retain his pride.

Before I went into the meeting I was sent a prepared statement and asked to put my name to it. In return for doing that, I was told the summons would be dropped. But it read like it had been written by The Sandy Easdale Fan Club. I looked it over and said: "No. I won't sign that. It's all lies. Just sue me." I hadn't actually said anything. It was other people's opinions about him plus facts about things that had previously happened in his life.

I will be honest, I did actually get on with Sandy to a degree. You could talk to him. He was similar to me in many respects. But I couldn't put out a statement saying he was a great guy who was fantastic for the club because I didn't think that was the case. In the days after the meeting we came up with a statement which was agreeable to both of us.

I was asking him for all sorts of things. I sensed that if I had asked for the team to play in a pink and purple polka dot away strip he would have agreed to it. I told him I would like to take a group of disabled and handicapped kids on a tour of Ibrox and Murray Park and he agreed.

In the days after our Stenhousemuir protest I received a direct message on Facebook from a Rangers fan called Stevie Sinclair. He wrote: "Look, I sort of get what you are trying to do. I am not for you or against you. But could you answer some questions I have?"

He raised some sensible points so I tried to address them.

At the Ayr United game that Saturday I found myself standing outside Somerset Park with a box of leaflets next to a Rangers fan in a wheelchair and his pal. I was looking at my Facebook page on my mobile phone as they chatted.

The guy said to his friend: "What do you think of those Sons of Struth guys? Are they right or wrong?"

His mate replied: "I don't know if we can believe them. But if they're right it's a bit scary what's going on at our club."

"I asked the guy a couple of questions and he responded and was quite open and honest. I think there is some truth in what they are saying."

At this point I tapped him on the shoulder, showed him my phone and asked: "Is that the message you sent me? How are you doing? I'm Craig."

We had a chat and have been friends ever since. Stevie isn't shy. If he thought we had done something wrong he would tell me. I respected him for that. I got told what we are doing was stupid all the time from a lot of different sources. None of it bothered me. But if somebody like Stevie, who was behind the general ethos of what we were doing, criticised us then I paid attention to that.

He had campaigned himself and done a lot of good work for the Thalidomide Society. He knew how PLC companies worked and how protests worked because he had organised them himself. He is savvy. He runs his own businesses. He is a good lad and quite an opinionated guy. When we took a group of disabled supporters for a tour of Auchenhowie and Ibrox he helped me organise it.

Sandy Easdale walked away from our meeting understanding one thing. I explained to him that it was impractical for me to monitor the Sons of Struth Facebook page constantly. But we agreed if he saw anything he was unhappy with then we would talk like human beings. He needed to get out of that predicament.

I stood my ground. I had the upper hand. I backed him into a corner. The reactions to the story online and at the next home game were a good indicator of what a dim view the Rangers support took of it. The very fact the fighting fund had spoken about paying my legal fees helped too. It all went berserk.

I put out a statement thanking the fans for their support. I also made it public that I would have voted against the fighting fund meeting the cost of my legal fees. There was a reaction to that suggestion. People said: "That wasn't what the money was for!" I actually agreed with that viewpoint. But I certainly thought it was a tremendous gesture for them to even contemplate it and I was touched.

They weren't the only ones who tried to help. I had three people come up to me at the ground when I was handing out leaflets and offer to remortgage their homes to pay my legal fees. One of them was close to me, one of them I had known less than a year and one of them was a complete stranger.

The last guy came up and said to me: "Listen son, I've looked into this, I reckon I could get you £50,000. But it'll take me about 10 days to get it." I had only asked him if he wanted a leaflet. That was the response I got!

I go to a Rangers matches now and people recognise me. It has its good points and its bad points. One of the good things is if somebody has a query about what is going on at the club then they can come and ask me. I am always happy to speak to them. But it can get embarrassing sometimes. On occasion, people have asked to get their photograph taken with me. My response is: "Eh? Why?" But I always oblige.

But people could send you messages online and pat you on the back going into the ground. None of them would have known the dark places my mind was at times. They would have no idea what a lift it gave me. It would really pull me out of a depressed state.

The blue card game was mad in that respect. People were coming up to me saying: "Don't let that bastard win Craig!" Hardly a person walked past me that day without making a comment. When somebody who was totally unknown to me walked past and offered to remortgage their house I was blown away. I couldn't walk 100 yards without somebody stopping me and offering their support, telling me not to give up or saying: "Who the hell does this guy think he is?"

It wasn't Craig Houston they were backing. It was just one of their own they were rallying behind. If, as has sadly been the case, a Rangers fan dies at a game or passes away in tragic circumstances then the support takes it personally. They grieve for them collectively.

An Aberdeen fan even sent me a message of support. That was more surprising than the Celtic fan. There were also followers of Hearts, St. Mirren and Kilmarnock. And Liverpool fans also got in touch.

I think my battle struck a chord with people. Modern football bears no resemblance to what it was like when I started following Rangers as a child. We aren't the only fans to feel disenfranchised from their club. There are numerous examples of that happening. At Cardiff a new owner took over and changed the colour of the strip and changed the badge. You wonder: "Do these people actually care about us?"

You would think that now a football club has become a multi-million pound business that you would, at the very least, be regarded as a customer. But no business in the world treated its customers the way Rangers did.

Dave King said something when the supporters met him once that made me think. He said: "You're a captive audience." He is right. If you don't like Asda you can drive a few miles along the road to Tesco. But once you are a Rangers fan you are a Rangers fan. You can't stop being a Rangers fan.

The truce I reached with Sandy Easdale wasn't an end to me being threatened with legal action. But the emails from his lawyer Peter Watson were less aggressive in their tone. They would read: "Craig, it has been pointed out that comment X has been made by poster Y." I would take it down and reply: "Sorry for the offence caused." Before that I was being threatened quite heavily.

I do like a laugh now and again. Sandy Chugg had served a stretch in prison. I put together a post that read: "Sandy is a crook. Sandy is a criminal. Sandy has been to jail." When people were reading it they must have thought it referred to Sandy Easdale. When you opened it up and got to the bottom it finished: "But Sandy Chugg is my best pal!"

To be fair to Sandy Easdale, he got it. He actually said that to me when I approached him in the directors' box. He knew we were taking the piss out of him. And we did. We took the complete and utter piss out of him. That is probably what made him take us to court.

I am certain that Sandy Easdale himself had no desire to sue me. I believe that his lawyer and PR man did. The reaction to some of the things they did was 180 degrees away from where they wanted it to be. But I thought what they did was foolish. Questioning supporters' loyalty to their club. Suing a fan. It was ridiculous. It is almost like they had read a book about how to attract bad publicity.

CHAPTER 11

DUPED

*"If you're loyal and you support the club then come out
and support the club. It doesn't matter who's running it.
I would ask every loyal Rangers fan, and I pick my words
correctly in saying loyal Rangers fans, supports the club
at this time and gives it a chance. We don't want to go
back to the dark days of administration."*

Sandy Easdale, Rangers football board chairman

THE possibility of withholding season ticket money from Rangers
and pooling it in some sort of bank account until the board gave
supporters a legal guarantee over Ibrox was first discussed by Billy
Montgomery and I shortly after the AGM in December of 2013.

Billy went away and did some research into what would be
involved. He spent weeks looking into it. As he was doing so, he
also sounded out some ex-players, former managers and well-
known supporters to see if any of them would be prepared to be
a figurehead for such a scheme. He knew a lot of the people he
spoke to personally. But he kept hitting a brick wall.

Billy put his findings to a Sons of Struth meeting in our usual
venue at the Ivory Hotel in February. We were all in agreement
that it was something worth pursuing. But we all felt that we
needed a big name to front it and we hadn't experienced any
joy on that front.

So I suggested the Union of Fans – a moniker for an amalgamation
of six supporters' groups I had come up with in the run-up to the
AGM the previous year – front it.

The Sons of Struth, who at that time essentially consisted of Sandy Chugg and I, had been receiving a growing number of plaudits for our actions. But we were getting a lot of help from a lot of people who were members of other groups. I wanted us to display some unity and was keen for everyone involved to be recognised.

Members of the three main club-approved supporters' bodies, the assembly, the association and the trust, were very active in the Sons of Struth. So, too, were members the Blue Order and the Union Bears who fill the singing sections at Ibrox and get the atmosphere going on match days. It was a good blend. Everybody had different strengths. We all contributed something.

There was only one other group, The Vanguard Bears, and they wanted to remain independent. But I felt getting six groups to come together was very positive. It really upsets me when I read that horrible word "factions" in connection with the Rangers fans. For me, there are no factions. We all support Rangers. We just have slightly different opinions about the board.

Now, I wasn't naive enough to think that everybody among the Rangers support thought our actions were fantastic. But I do think we proved beyond doubt with the blue and red card displays which we held at Ibrox that the majority of supporters approved with the majority of things we did.

People allege there is no unity among the Rangers support. The Union of Fans, an amalgamation of six supporters groups, was about as unified as we could get.

The Union of Fans had connotations with the Scottish independence referendum as well. Most Rangers fans were opposed to breaking away from the United Kingdom, were pro-Union and voted No. So we thought it would appeal to them.

We had produced a graphic in the build-up to the AGM which read: "The Union of Fans vote No." But, other than that, we hadn't done much with the name. I put forward the suggestion that the body should front the plan to withhold season ticket money and it was agreed. Within 24 hours we had set up a website, drawn up a media release and were preparing to hold a media conference.

One of the three aims of the Sons of Struth was to protect Ibrox. That was declared long before the club started using assets like

Edmiston House and the Albion Car Park to secure loans. From the very outset, we were afraid the stadium would be used for the same purpose. We were worried if it was and if the club entered into administration again there was a very real chance it could actually be lost.

We were certain the club was on the verge of using Murray Park as security because we had been told valuations had been carried out by sources we had within the club. Several employees confirmed to us independently of each other that companies had been commissioned to carry out the work. The information we received suggested it was a done deal.

It was more of a general sense of foreboding with Ibrox. We didn't think they could possibly pawn off the stadium. We knew there would be uproar if they did so. But there was a nagging suspicion there so we acted on it. Because it was one of the main aims of Sons of Struth we felt we had to do something.

That apprehension was the driving force behind looking to secure Ibrox. We felt that if we managed to put a few million pounds for season tickets into a kitty of some kind we could use it as leverage in negotiations with the board to protect the stadium.

THE blue card display we had held at the SPFL League One game against Dunfermline at Ibrox on March 15 was designed to encourage the board to enter into meaningful negotiations with Dave King. He had stated he was prepared to invest substantial sums, tens of millions of pounds, in return for representation on the board. We felt that was preferable to short-term loan deals.

It read: "Hold up this card in the 18th and 72nd minutes if you want to support Dave King's attempts to invest much needed money into Rangers. Use your power as fans for positive change. We need investment and trusted figures on the board now. Support Dave King. We need investment."

Probably the same number of people joined in with the blue card protest as had joined in with the red card protest. But the impact was far greater. It was strange. It may have had something to do with the contrast with the crowd colour or the seat colour. Whatever the reason, it was very powerful.

Because the game was being shown on Sky Sports, instead of distributing the blue cards at the turnstiles around the ground evenly we decided to concentrate on the three stands away from the main stand. We focused on the Broomloan Road Stand, the Copland Road Stand and the Govan Stand, what is now the Sandy Jardine Stand, because they would be seen by the television cameras.

But when the cards first went up in the 18th minute, thousands of people in the three tiers of the main stand had them. We had received quite a lot of publicity in the media in the build-up to the protest and that helped. Everybody going to the game was aware of what was going on. Many people actively sought us out to get them. I was posted outside the Copland that day. There were fans coming up to us and saying: "Can I take a pile of them to hand out?" The cards made their way around the four corners of the stadium. It looked fantastic and was a great success.

King came over to Scotland the week before the display and was in the country, although not at the game, when it was staged. He flew in to hold talks with the board. But he also met with selected fans on two occasions during his visit. The usual suspects – Gordon Dinnie, Mark Dingwall, Chris Graham, Billy Montgomery, Tam Green, James Riddell, myself and others - were invited to an office in Glasgow city centre to speak to him the day before the game.

He explained to us that his plan was to invest between £20 million and £30 million personally. He told us he was going to talk with the board about doing so. He also revealed he had meetings set up with other interested parties and wealthy individuals who he felt may be prepared to put money into the club.

Then he asked us to turn the volume down. I had misgivings about that. I said to him: "Any occasion we've backed off in the past it has given the club time. They've tended to regroup and come out of it rosy." I added: "I'm quite good at organising protests and annoying directors. I trust that you're good in board rooms. I hope you're right and you've read this correctly."

King met with the board members over that weekend and was far from impressed. Indeed, he came back on Monday and told us in no uncertain terms how awful his encounter with the club directors had been. Some of them had taken umbrage at his probing questions and been quite aggressive towards him.

My Gran "Nana". Isa Houston didn't make me a Rangers fan, but she taught me about the history and standards of the club.

From left to right, my dad, me and my sister Fiona.

East Fulton Primary School, Linwood. The boys in three of the four corners were all part of Sons of Struth. Top left is David Adam, bottom left is Stewart Campbell and I am bottom right.

David Adam and I enjoying a ferocious game of Crossfire. I am wearing my favourite ever Rangers away top.

Back row, from left to right, me, Scott Campbell, my cousin Alec and Stewart Campbell. Bottom row, from left to right, my cousins Darren and Brian Reilly, who respectfully wore Liverpool tracksuits instead of their normal Celtic ones for this birthday celebration and an unknown girl.

Robert McCarron and I with my East Fulton Primary School team kit on. Hopefully my bedroom décor confirms that, contrary to what some people say, I have always been a bear.

Linwood Rangers on tour in Cleethorpes. Myself (with hand on ball), Derek Whittington (goalie) and Gavin McCallum (centre front row to my left). Both of them were part of SOS. Good Bear Henry "Two Thumbs" Wotherspoon is also there.

The "Striking Miners", winners of annual Linwood five-a-side competition. The name came about due to the miner's strike being on at the time. I am in the front row on the left with my tie on, Derek Whittington is behind me and Alex Marshall is beside me. We were all delighted as John Greig presented us with our trophies. The other three are not as happy. It was a mixed team. Kevin Lee, with the large trophy, went to St. Mirren as a young professional.

SONS OF STRUTH DEMAND THE TRUTH

With Drummy Bear at Silloth with the Drumsagard Football Academy.
Happy days

Sons of Struth select v Armed Forces Veterans team. The SOS team, in black and white, included my son Ben (top row second from the left), myself (top row fifth from right),, Justin Currie from the District Bar (top row third from right) and Sandy Chugg (front row fourth from right) with his son Nathan (who is a better goalie than his dad). The Forces team had John Noble (front row, third from left) who became a good friend and will lead the soon to be SOS VFC, a team for army veterans.

Me, Ibrox tunnel area.

Willie Vass

SONS OF STRUTH DEMAND THE TRUTH

Craig Whyte.
Not my favourite Rangers chairman

SOS letting James and Sandy Easdale and
Graham Wallace know what we demand
from them.

I am to the left of the "DEMAND THE TRUTH" banner. Brian Bowman in the centre of the "SPIVS OUT" banner looks like
he has the longest arms in the world.

Another day another protest. Sandy and I are in the middle here. Sandy has his daughter on his shoulders and his son by his side. Les Henderson and Michael Grover are at the end of the banner. Ian McColl from the Founders Trail is second from the left.

Sons of Struth didn't do breaks at the end of the season. We delivered our postcards telling the board what they had to do before we would buy our season tickets.

SONS OF STRUTH DEMAND THE TRUTH

Outside the famous blue gates during the postcard demo.

Rangers fans really are the people.

From left to right, John Brown, Iain Ferguson and Nacho Novo. Former players from three different eras joined us for the protest before the Hibs game. We didn't go in, we were boycotting by this time

The scenes from inside the stadium at pre-match demonstration against Hearts. This was one of the biggest crowds we pulled. The bears had said "enough was enough".

SONS OF STRUTH DEMAND THE TRUTH

The blue card display to show support of Dave King.

The blue card.

The postcard demo. Delivering our message.

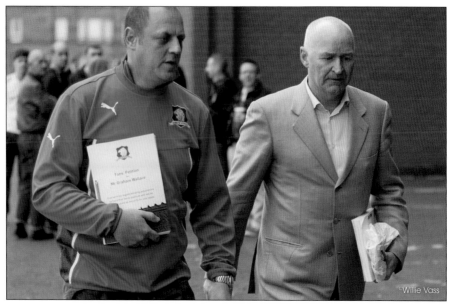

John Brown delivered a petition saying "enough is enough" to the board on behalf of the Rangers fans. This was his first, but not his last involvement with SOS.

March 6, 2015 - the day we got our club back. John Gilligan, Dave King and Paul Murray look pretty happy.

Left to right, David Adam, myself, John MacDonald, Stewart Campbell and Scott Campbell celebrating the AGM victory in the District Bar. I was told by many I had a great night that night. I will take their word for it. The Campbell brothers and I had met John 30 or so years previously when he was playing for the club. We didn't have a camera that day. We got there in the end.

Rangers fans doing what we also wanted to do, supporting our club

My Dad and I in the director's box. My dad went from eating programmes that night to eating pies. David Leggat and Mark Dingwall in front of us.

Nan Laurie, the Duchess of Copland Road, before a game. A true lady with a great family.

From left to right, myself, Sandy Chugg and Chris Bates celebrating something or other. I can't remember much about that night other than waking up in Sandys couch. Our host Simba gave us a good night.

It was great to take a group of kids on a tour of Ibrox and visit the first team training. Wee James in front of me became a great pal after this tour. Love the wee man to bits.

Sandy, myself and Brian Miller, all Drumsagard coaches, after a 10k run to raise funds for the kids.

Michael Mols, myself and Marco Negri. Two heroes of mine who later became ambassadors for the Sons of Struth Football Academy.

Colin Stein, Davie Wilson, Willie Johnston and I all at a tribute night for Davie at Ibrox

Graeme Souness and Richard Gough either side of me. Can you get better company?

The Lewis and Harris RSC honoured myself (SOS), Chris Graham (Rangers Supporters Trust) and Ricki Neill (Rangers First) at their annual Player of the Year awards. The largest Rangers supporters club in the world had ex-players John Brown and Charlie Miller present us with our awards. Their committee decided we had done more than any player that year.

He admitted he was wrong about turning the noise down. He said they deserved everything they got.

Gordon, the chairman of the Rangers Supporters Trust, asked how his meetings with the other interested parties had gone and enquired whether they wanted to put money in. He told us that some had said they would be prepared to invest if he gained control. Others hadn't wanted to invest at the level he had hoped they would.

Gordon then asked if the figure he had hoped to invest that he had mentioned on the Friday – between £20 million and £30 million – had altered. King assured us he would make up the shortfall personally. We all left happy with a guy who had the same feelings about the board as us.

I always try to make things as simple as I possibly can. For me, everything is usually pretty black and white. There were some fairly awful things said about Dave King during his lengthy legal battle with the South African Revenue Service over a tax bill. He was called a "glib and shameless liar" and "a mendacious witness" by a judge during that lengthy process.

He went through that over a period of 11 years and then paid a sum of £43.7 million after being found guilty of 41 counts of breaching the South African Income Tax Act in August 2013.

You can view that however you like. But, for me, it was interesting that he continued to conduct business in South Africa, own companies in South Africa and sit on the board of directors of companies in South Africa after that. Why did the authorities in that country allow him to do that if he was this master criminal many painted him as?

There is a section of Scottish society who didn't want Dave King to be involved with Rangers because they believed Dave King may have been good for Rangers. There were even some people in the media who I believed felt that way as well. But my argument was: "How can he continue to operate in the country where he experienced these tax issues?"

We were ready to announce our season ticket boycott towards the end of April. Then, just before we were set to launch it, we received word that Dave King was poised to do exactly the same thing. We were asked to abort our plan to enable him to launch his vehicle - which we could then declare our support for.

My feelings at the time, and I wasn't alone within the Union of Fans on this, was that we should proceed as planned and let him endorse us. But when you have a committee you have to go with what the majority want and I was outvoted on that issue.

So Dave King unveiled Ibrox 1972 on the Wednesday and we got behind him on the Thursday. Our website was only online for a day before it changed to support the scheme he set up. The public would have seen it as his idea which the fans had lent their backing to. But we had set the wheels in motion to do the same thing long before he turned up.

As I say, I was of the opinion the fans should have taken the lead and King should have supported us, not the other way around. But there were advantages to the way it panned out. There were significant monetary costs involved which he took care of. I am reliably informed it personally set him back around £100,000.

Most of that was spent on legal fees and ensuring the terms were worded correctly. We had to know we could use people's money for the purpose we wanted to use it for. So the positives were that Dave King footed the bill and it was watertight. That was important.

The Rangers Fans Fighting Fund was set up with good intentions when the club went into administration in 2012 to raise money to help the club in its fight for survival. But it was done in a hurry. There is now a pile of cash, roughly £500,000, sitting gathering dust in a bank vault. It is harder to spend it now than it was to raise at the time because of the complex legal issues involved. We didn't want to be caught in the same trap.

Oddly enough, when the club finally started season ticket renewals, they failed to attract a card payment merchant. That was due, chief executive Graham Wallace revealed in the findings of his 120 day review in April, to payment processor First Data wanting security over Ibrox in return for their services due to "negative publicity" surrounding the club. The club wasn't prepared to grant that. So they were unable to accept credit and debit card payments. But Ibrox 1972, as a newly-formed company without any such issues, was.

Interestingly, emails from First Data to senior officials at Rangers – including Graham Wallace - which showed the company had requested full security the month before Dave King had launched Ibrox 1972 were consequently leaked to the Daily Record and published the day after the findings of the review were released.

We didn't actually receive a penny. All we did was ask Rangers fans to pledge their season ticket money to us. The plan was to use their support during talks with the club. Then, once they agreed to our demands, we would hit a button and call in the money.

When I had my meeting with Graham Wallace in February we had discussed lots of things. But a season ticket boycott wasn't raised once. I was certain he would ask me about it. But he had just received the results of his "Ready to Listen" survey of Rangers supporters. They showed that only five per cent of those polled were part of an official fans organisation. The club hierarchy pounced on that. In fact, I knew from sources inside the club they were absolutely delighted with it. I think they felt: "Even if every one of these guys doesn't renew their ticket it isn't that bad". They thought a couple of thousand might do it.

At the end of our meeting I said: "You haven't asked about the season ticket boycott." The impression I got was that they really weren't concerned. It was clear they didn't believe it would get the backing that it did. As I was leaving, I turned to him and said: "Believe me, you will phone me about this. We'll have to speak about it at some point."

In the weeks after Ibrox 1972 was set up information from within the club about how many season tickets had been sold filtered through to us. We updated how many season tickets were sold on the Sons of Struth Facebook page. One week it was 7,000. The next week it was 9,000. But, as always with a source, we were only 99.9 per cent certain the information we were getting was accurate. There was always that bit of doubt.

Somebody would post online that 20,000 or 25,000 had been sold. Bill McMurdo, the football agent's son of the same name who wrote a blog which was very supportive of the regime at Ibrox, was one of them. So there was always that bit of uncertainty. The doubt grew as time went on.

Halfway through the renewal period I got a phone call from Al Lamont at BBC Scotland. He told me he was going to doorstep Sandy Easdale as he went in to a meeting at Ibrox that morning and ask him some questions about season ticket sales. He wanted to know if I could give a supporter's response to his comments later on. I agreed to do it. But I was suspicious.

I thought: "I've been kicked out of Ibrox twice for doing interviews with the BBC?" Jonathan Sutherland had interviewed me one day. They were filming me walking along Edmiston Drive in front of the main stand. The cameraman had his foot on the front step. Somebody swiftly came out and informed us the BBC were banned and told us to beat it. So we shuffled up the street to the blue gate. We were ordered to move along again.

I asked myself: "How can Al Lamont stand outside Argyle House without getting flung out? How can he say with any confidence he is going to interview Sandy Easdale in particular?" To me, when you doorstep a meeting you speak to everybody involved in the hope that one or more of them stops and speaks to you. That suggested to me it was a pre-arranged interview.

Al called back later and told me, surprise, surprise, he had spoken to Sandy and asked me to pop down to the BBC studios at Pacific Quay to talk to him. I was dumbstruck when I heard the interview. In it Sandy had questioned the loyalty of Rangers fans several times. He had stated the club's finances were in a fragile state. He said the club was in danger. He also denied knowing anything about a season ticket boycott. It was incredible.

He said: "If you're loyal and you support the club then come out and support the club. It doesn't matter who's running it. I would ask every loyal Rangers fan, and I pick my words correctly in saying loyal Rangers fans, supports the club at this time and gives it a chance. We don't want to go back to the dark days of administration."

I did the interview - and got quite heated. I also went on radio later that evening with Michael Grant of The Herald and Richard Wilson of the BBC. Al did an interview over the phone on the show. It became obvious during the course of it that he was still up at Ibrox. So I decided to head up there after we had finished.

I wanted to try and catch Sandy Easdale. In the five minute drive to the stadium I received two phone calls from pals who had listened to me. I told both of them: "Look, I can't talk, I'm driving up to Ibrox. I've got a horrible feeling in my stomach."

One of them went away and posted that on one of the supporters' internet forums. He started a thread titled: "Craig Houston is heading up to Ibrox." I had been up there for 10 minutes when more fans started arriving. Pretty quickly, there were about a dozen folk there. Before long there were around 50 or so.

There were a lot of concerned supporters. They were coming up to me and saying: "Craig, what are you doing? Are you here to see Sandy Easdale? Are we going into administration tonight?" What can only be described as an angry mob had soon gathered.

When Sandy finally came out of Argyle House I went over to confront him. When he was about 50 yards away from me and about to get into his car I shouted out his name and he turned round. Roughly translated, his body language when he spotted me said: "Oh fuck! Not you again!"

But, to be fair to him, we shook hands as we started our conversation, as we always did, and we shook hands as we finished our conversation, as we always did. I hauled him up about questioning the loyalty of Rangers fans. His response was: "He caught me in the heat of the moment. I didn't mean it that way. I was just caught on the hop." I replied: "Bollocks!"

There were two reasons I knew that was rubbish. One, the interview was a set-up. Two, he had said it more than once. Now I am no media relations guru. But one thing I quickly realised after I started doing interviews myself was that when you had a prepared message you often ended up repeating it. If you wanted to make a specific point you would say it two or three times. It is in the back of your mind. I was in no doubt his comments had been pre-prepared by somebody else.

Then I said: "You've also said that you don't know anything about our season ticket boycott. Funny how you're quick enough to phone me when you see things online that you aren't happy with. Why don't you give me a call some time and I'll explain to you what it is?" He said he would and left. He didn't call.

The only man still left in the building was poor Graham Wallace who had nothing to do with the interview. Although he wasn't my favourite person, I did think: "I wouldn't like to be him just now." He had to come out to face a baying mob to answer questions about a situation which he hadn't created.

I started getting phone calls telling me there were rumours circulating that Sandy Jardine, who had been battling cancer for a long time, had passed away. That was obviously terrible to hear. But it made me wary. It would have reflected badly on the supporters if there had been any unrest at the stadium on the night that a Rangers legend like Sandy died.

I was very worried about what would happen if Graham Wallace came out to go to his car and was accosted or confronted. If anything, God forbid, was to happen to him it would have looked awful if it had been picked up on in the media.

Graham Wallace's secretary, who I had met and spoken to on numerous occasions by that stage, had come out of Argyle House and was standing there speaking to Sandy Chugg who had also arrived. She said: "Craig, Mr Wallace would like to speak to you." I said: "I think that would be a very good idea."

I went in and spent half an hour chatting with him in his office. He was clearly, although he didn't say as much outright, upset the interview had taken place. He was annoyed at several of the statements which had been made during it. He didn't agree with them. He told me they were inaccurate.

I asked him if he was happy with the situation and he failed to respond. That in itself told me that he wasn't. I told him I thought the interview had been stage managed. I asked: "If it wasn't our PR department who arranged it who was it?" I was pretty sure it was Jack Irvine – who wasn't meant to be working for anybody involved with Rangers.

I said to Graham: "You've still not spoken to me about this boycott." He replied: "I'll speak to you about it soon." To his credit, he was, unlike Sandy Easdale, true to his word and did call. While sitting there we received confirmation that Sandy Jardine had passed away. I went outside and broke the news to the people outside.

There was obviously going to be a minute's silence and other tributes to Sandy Jardine at the game against Stranraer at Ibrox that Saturday. There was no way we would hold a protest that day. We had got 40,000 red cards printed off. But most of them are sitting unused in a lock-up in Glasgow. We have probably only used around 5,000 or so of them.

We took them to Dunfermline for the final game of the season the following week and held a protest in the away stand. We also took them out when we held a postcard protest the next summer. But not being able to use them as we had originally intended didn't matter. It paled into insignificance next to the passing of an all-time Rangers great.

The night the news broke that Sandy Jardine had died Graham Wallace told me the 120 day review he had pledged to carry out when he was appointed was complete. He said: "I think you'll like what's in it." When it was published the following day I read it all and had no idea what I was supposed to be impressed by.

He must have thought that coming clean on what had gone on, how much money had been frittered away in the previous two years – the figure given was a staggering £67.2 million - and the onerous contracts the club was tied to would satisfy fans.

But it was poppycock. How it took 128 days to come up with was beyond me. It said virtually nothing. There was no plan in place going forward. The strategy still seemed to be the one that the former finance director Brian Stockbridge had put forward after the club released its audited accounts in 2013.

Stockbridge was interviewed by Andrew Dickson of Rangers TV and was asked: "What is your plan?" He responded: "To ensure the club is financially secure and to move back to the top of Scottish football as quick as we possibly can." If I had come away with that when I was running car showrooms I would have been huckled out of the door in jig time.

For me, there was no substance to the business review. It stated the club needed money. No shit Sherlock! But it didn't say where it was coming from.

The 120 day business review could have been done in a week. You only really had two income streams. One was punters and the other was sponsorship. There wasn't much revenue from broadcasting. There wasn't much prize money either. To find where the money was coming in and was exiting wouldn't have taken long.

Taking over four months to come up with a business plan - which, by the way, didn't present much of a plan other than saying "we want to do as well as we possibly can" - meant they bought time after the AGM. Everybody was waiting with bated breath to see what they came up with.

The noisy minority of people who backed the board online were always looking to something on the horizon. First it would be: "We'll wait until the accounts come out." They came out and they were terrible. Then people said: "We'll wait until the AGM." That happened and the board was re-elected en masse at a farce of a meeting. Then it was: "We will wait until the 120 day business review is published." They kept moving the finishing post.

If Graham Wallace had intimated to me in Feburary when I had met him or subsequently informed supporters that he wasn't being allowed to do his job then he would have received the full backing of Sons of Struth and in turn the Union of Fans.

But he chose to tell me he was the man who was making the decisions. So for that reason he had to be held accountable. All he had to do was put his hand out. But he sided with the bad guys. It was dead simple. It was good versus evil, cowboys v Indians, Jedi Knights v Imperial Stormtroopers. You were either on one side or the other. For me, you had to make it black and white for the fans.

He could have chosen a different part for himself in the whole pantomime. He decided not to and ended up being bracketed with Sandy Easdale and David Somers as a result. But instead of going out and recruiting support from the supporters they stayed within the confines of the boardroom. It was impossible for anyone to help him.

When I met with Graham Wallace in February I did say to him: "It doesn't have to be made public that you're being held back from doing your job. But if we know that is the case we will work on that basis." But he said: "I am not being prevented from doing anything." I knew, the fans knew and probably the dugs in the street knew that he was. But he felt he was strong enough.

I am convinced that, right up to the death, he didn't feel that Jack Irvine was working on behalf of Sandy Easdale. But there was a campaign to discredit him. It was revealed by Bill McMurdo that he had received a £160,000 bonus and it was claimed he was looking for the full £350,000 in October 2014.

Ally McCoist was the first manager in the history of the club to have his wages made public. Now, whether he got paid too much or too little is a different argument. What is key is that it worked. People latched onto it. He looked bad in front of the people who had supported him when he stood by the club. There was a campaign to get rid of the manager a year before he left.

Fans should have been asking different questions. Did anybody know what Stuart McCall's wages were when he came in as interim manager for the end of the 2014/15 season? No. Did anybody know what Kenny McDowall's remuneration was when he was in charge before that? Not that I knew of. But with Ally McCoist it was different. It was leaked to undermine him. For me, the information should have been across the board.

I must admit to being disappointed at the number of journalists who accepted phone calls and published information which was fed to them by Jack Irvine. I didn't think they should have been taking stories off him because he didn't represent Rangers. They would tell me he was saying this or that to them. I would ask: "Why are you buying into this?"

AS we were getting closer to the season ticket renewal deadline, we did a lot of publicity work with former players. The likes of Lorenzo Amoruso, John Brown, Richard Gough and others got involved and we received a lot of coverage in the newspapers, on radio and on television. But there was still no contact from the club. So I started emailing, texting and phoning Graham Wallace several times a day asking when he was going to speak to me.

I did start to think: "Maybe we've got our figures wrong here. If they're as low as we believe they are then surely he'd want to speak to us." As time went on, we were being told from inside the club that only 14,000 or 15,000 season tickets had been sold. That was a huge drop on the 36,000 or so who had bought them the season before. But I started to seriously doubt that our actions were having the impact that we hoped they would.

Then one Friday morning around a week before the deadline my mobile rang. The number calling came up as "Graham Wallace". I knew before I even answered that our figures were spot on. Right enough, I answered and he said: "Craig, we need to talk."

I went on to have a series of telephone conversations with him throughout May. During one of them, he told me: "You're never going to get security for the ground. It can't happen. There are legal reasons, business reasons, for that." But that in no way deterred us. I replied: "There has to be a happy medium. We have to negotiate and meet somewhere in the middle."

I think Graham Wallace was under the impression that Chris Graham and Chris Graham alone was the Union of Fans. Chris had certainly done an amazing amount of work setting up Ibrox 1972 and arranging the boycott of season tickets. He put a lot of time and effort into it. He works in finance so it made perfect sense for him to take care of that. I told him: "It's not just Chris, it's an amalgamation of six groups and a lot of people are involved."

But he seemed encouraged when I informed him I had created it and could speak to those who formed it. Eventually he told me: "I can get you a full, written, legal guarantee that we won't sell Ibrox. I can't do the same for Auchenhowie. But I'm quite happy to cede to your demands on the stadium. Can you get approval on that offer from the guys on the Union of Fans?" I told him: "I don't think that will be an issue Graham."

We both agreed to adopt the role of Kofi Annan with our respective organisations. As I understood it, Graham was going to speak to the Rangers board and make sure they agreed to the proposal. I, meanwhile, was going speak to the representatives on the Union of Fans to get them onside. Then we would hold a meeting with a few representatives from both sides present where the arrangement would be finalised.

It wasn't difficult for me. I spoke to everybody I needed to by the Monday and Tuesday. They were all in favour of it. The meeting was arranged on the Wednesday night at Ibrox. It should all have been so straightforward. It turned out to be anything but.

Chris Graham, Gordon Dinnie and Drew Roberton went along as the representatives of the Union of Fans, the Rangers Supporters Trust and the Rangers Supporters Association respectively. I went with my Sons of Struth hat on.

Graham Wallace was a bit funny about Chris Graham coming. The Union of Fans had released a statement calling for him to be sacked for allegedly misleading comments he had made. He had stood up at the AGM in December and insisted the club had enough money to keep it afloat for the remainder of the 2013/14 season.

Then in February the Rangers board announced they had agreed two emergency loans -which were secured on Edmiston House and the Albion Car Park - worth £1.5 million with Sandy Easdale and Laxey Partners for working capital. Sandy had declined to accept interest on his loan. But Laxey stood to make £150,000 in the space of six months. There was, not surprisingly, a furious reaction from supporters.

At that point, Ibrox and Auchenhowie were the only security we had left. We felt completely justified in the course of action we were taking after that. It strengthened the desire to secure the future of the stadium. We felt: "Well, what's next?"

I could actually understand Wallace's misgivings about Chris to a degree. But I told him: "The Union is a group of people, Chris is just the spokesman. We all agreed on the wording of the release. It just so happened that it was his name on it." He backed down.

Sitting there in the boardroom at Argyle House with my group of ragamuffin friends on the night of the meeting waiting for the Rangers directors to arrive was another one of the many surreal moments I experienced. I thought: "A year ago these guys didn't know my name and I didn't know their names - and now I'm sitting in the boardroom at Ibrox about to hold a meeting with them about the future of the stadium."

I was struck by the poor condition of the room. The seats we were sitting on were worn and torn. The decor was tired. It was in desperate need of a lick of paint. I dread to think what potential investors or sponsors would have thought of the place if they sat there. It gave a really bad impression. It was the scruffiest board room I have ever been in and I have been in a few. It saddened me.

Norman Crighton, Sandy Easdale and Graham Wallace duly arrived. We all introduced ourselves and the meeting got underway. Quite early on, Wallace raised his concerns about Chris and some of the comments he had made about him in the newspapers. Straight away, I said: "Look Graham, we're not here to talk about you, we're not here to talk about Chris, we're not here to talk about the statement. We're here to talk about Rangers, Ibrox and this fund."

But he persevered. He admitted he found it difficult to sit at the same table as someone who had made such serious allegations about him. He had been reported to the police for his comments at the AGM. I said to him: "Listen, I'm sitting at the same table as somebody who tried to sue me for £200,000 not so long ago!" There were a few chortles at that comment. I suggested he just accept Chris's presence and move on.

Sandy Easdale had a terrible habit of talking about Sandy Easdale whenever he met with Rangers supporters. It was all about Sandy Easdale with Sandy Easdale. I think he just wanted a cuddle and to be told everything was going to be alright. Almost inevitably, he then piped up with a question he must have asked about 100 times. He said: "How come nobody likes me?"

Chris responded immediately. He said: "I'll tell you why! Because you're a liar! You said in an interview with STV before the AGM that you had investors lined up. Then six weeks later we needed a loan to keep the club afloat and the doors open!"

Sandy said: "But I've covered that with big Craig!" He looked at me and added: "You tell him!"

He was referring to a discussion that had taken place between us at the meeting we had held at Ibrox earlier that year before which we had both signed a non-disclosure document to prevent us from talking publicly about it.

I replied: "Sandy, I can't tell him. Remember, you got me to sign a piece of paper so I wouldn't speak about what we said. So how can I tell Chris what was said?"

He said: "Just tell him, I won't have a problem with it."

"Well, you might not have a problem with it, you were certainly alright speaking to The Sun about it on the night of the meeting, but I refused to comment. So, no, I'm not talking about it. You're not on."

Graham Wallace interrupted. He said I was correct. He suggested to Sandy that it would be quicker if he just answered Chris's question about what happened to the investors he had lined up. What happened next was bonkers.

I thought: "I've already heard this so I don't have to listen to it all over again." I stood up and went to the side of the room where there was a table with tea, coffee and biscuits on it. I stuck a custard cream in my mouth and started pumping coffee out of the thermos into a cup. As I was doing this, Sandy started to give his explanation.

To my utter astonishment, it was completely different to what he had told me before. He said the investors had been put off by the actions of the fans and had pulled out. I nearly choked on my biscuit. When I had recovered my composure, I spat it out of my mouth, turned around and screamed: "What the fuck are you talking about Sandy! That's not what you told me. Stop telling fucking lies!"

Sandy said to me: "Well, what did I tell you before?"

I told him: "Sandy! I can't tell anybody what you said before! But rest assured that's a totally different answer you're giving!"

Eventually, things calmed down and we got down to the matter we were all there to discuss. We were negotiating over two points in that meeting. We were prepared to accept a written undertaking over the future of Ibrox over total security. We were also dropping the request for a similar commitment over the training ground at Auchenhowie. We felt we were conceding a lot.

But we decided beforehand that we would put a request for a guarantee over Auchenhowie back on the table. If they came back to us after they had held their board meeting and told us it wasn't possible – and, remember, we had been told the facilities and site had been valued – we would almost certainly have accepted it. We just thought we would chance it. Nothing ventured nothing gained was our attitude. We were also curious to see what the reaction of the directors was when we started talking about the training ground.

Norman Crighton's role in the negotiations was strange. He asked us how much was in our kitty. We told him there wasn't a penny. He asked us how much was going to be in it. We told him we weren't prepared to tell him due to the fact they hadn't told us how many season tickets the club had sold.

We were playing a game of poker. We didn't know what hand we had. We just hoped they believed that we held all of the aces. He suggested that Ibrox was worth a substantial amount of money. He argued that to justify giving security over it to us we would need to have a large sum.

I said: "Let's forget about Ibrox for a minute. You've told us you can't consider giving us security over the stadium. So how much is Auchenhowie worth? Wouldn't it be easier looking at the training ground?" His face turned about five different colours in as many seconds. He started stammering. I knew the reason for his discomfort. It had already been earmarked for something.

We hit him again. I said: "Did you just say you need to talk to shareholders before giving away security?" He confirmed that they had. I responded: "That's fine Mr Crighton. As the chairman of our investment committee, maybe you could enlighten us about which shareholders you asked before you gave out security over the Albion Car Park and Edmiston House." He changed colour several times once again. We knew the only shareholders he spoke to were Sandy Easdale, Laxey Partners, Blue Pitch Holdings and Margarita Funds Holding Trust.

He moved forward in his chair and started to voice his opinion quite strongly. He had, by all accounts, reacted the same way when Dave King asked him some quite tricky questions about the same loan. He responded: "Actually, now you mention it, I don't need to speak to shareholders. We didn't do it before. It was a board decision." I said: "Good, well you don't need to speak to any shareholders about what we're talking about."

I felt we had just played a winning hand. Ultimately, though, I was proved wrong.

We also put it to him that all he had done as chairman of the investment committee when the club was looking for a loan was speak to Sandy Easdale and his paymasters Laxey Partners.

He assured us that was not the case and insisted he had spoken to lots of different people. In his defence, he did come up with another name.

The message we received was that granting an undertaking over Ibrox wasn't a problem. Auchenhowie, meanwhile, would be discussed.

We did some simple arithmetic after that meeting. Two of the directors we had at the club at that time, Norman Crighton and Graham Wallace, were present. The others were James Easdale and David Somers. But as Sandy Easdale effectively spoke for his brother James we pretty much had three of the four directors there.

They were all happy to grant a legal undertaking over Ibrox. They told us their next course of action would be to have a board meeting the next day and get this passed. We expected it to be a brief discussion because the majority of the board had agreed in principle to what we were pushing for. The only thing up for debate was the future of the training ground. But that was by no means a deal breaker.

We came out of the stadium that night believing we were on the verge of reaching an agreement. We thought we had got what we were fighting for. We released a statement to the media on developments.

Graham Wallace had asked us before the meeting to keep it secret and we did so. It wasn't leaked to the newspapers and it didn't appear on social media. Then we were asked at the meeting if we wanted to keep what was discussed confidential. We explained that we couldn't do that. We were representing thousands of Rangers fans and we felt we needed to relay to them what had been discussed.

We were confident we were going to secure Ibrox for the Rangers fans. Not for the Sons of Struth or the Rangers Supporters Trust or the Union of Fans or the Rangers Supporters Association. For the Rangers fans. Every last one of them.

If supporters were reading newspaper stories on Thursday predicting a favourable outcome they could have said: "It's all sorted. I'll go and buy my season ticket tomorrow." I was certainly convinced myself that was the case.

But nothing happened.

No call came in. As the day wore on my stomach started churning. I thought of all of the supporters rushing out to buy season tickets on the understanding that a guarantee had been given over Ibrox. I could visualise them nicking up to the stadium during their lunch hour or after they finished work because they believed the supporters had won. It didn't sit right with me. I felt ill.

So I phoned Keith Jackson at the Daily Record. I said: "I need a favour. Could you write a piece urging Rangers fans not to buy season tickets tomorrow?" I seem to recall him swearing down the line at me.

Remember, Keith's newspaper, along with every other broadsheet and tabloid in Scotland, had run stories heralding the imminent outbreak of peace at Rangers that morning.

He said to me: "What for?"

I replied: "Because I think they've fucked us. I don't think they're going to do the deal. They might agree to it on Saturday, Sunday or Monday. But I can't run that risk. I can't have thousands of fans renew season tickets on the strength of a maybe. Help me. I need to do something."

"For fuck sake Craig! Have they lied to you? Hold on I'll get my pen."

The back page headline in the Record the next day was: "Sold A Dummy." The story underlined that no agreement had been reached. It was essentially a warning to anyone who was thinking of renewing. I would like to think it prevented a huge rise in season ticket sales on deadline day.

If I had been cynical I would have concluded the board had only agreed to the meeting in order to increase season ticket sales two days before the deadline. But two things suggested to me that wasn't the case. One, they asked us to keep the talks secret beforehand. And, two, they asked if the details of the discussions could remain private as we left the room.

If they had wanted to boost sales they wouldn't have requested confidentiality. They would have wanted everyone to know that everything had been settled. I'm convinced they had good intentions. Having been a salesman for over 20 years, I like to think I can read people's body language and sense when they are lying and when they are telling the truth. I am sure they were prepared to give a legally binding guarantee over Ibrox as they walked out that room.

I am also certain their minds were changed the following day. I believe the same shareholders who Norman Crighton had insisted the board didn't need to speak to were responsible for that.

If the board made the decision I would be shocked and stunned. Their job was to sell season tickets and get the club on an even keel. They could have sold 10,000, at the very least, on the back of the compromise we agreed upon.

I said something to Graham Wallace at the meeting. I said: "We've got something you want and you've got something we want. This situation can be beneficial to both parties. We could even sell season tickets through the credit and debit card facilities we have. You can't do that. We can work together on this. Give us the assurances we are looking for and we can give you an instant increase in your season ticket sales. We'll actually become your salesmen."

Not only could we sell to people who were holding back on renewing we could sell to people who couldn't actually physically buy season tickets. As a salesman, the final outcome just seemed ridiculous to me. A normal business in normal circumstances would not have, could not possibly have, knocked that deal back.

How could they turn down the opportunity to sell thousands of season tickets and bank millions of pounds just to give a written undertaking on an issue they had agreed to verbally? I am convinced that things were going on in the background which we weren't privy to. Was Mike Ashley's attempt to get the stadium as security months later the reason they changed their mind? I don't know.

We didn't hear another word from them. We didn't receive a phone call, an email or a text. They could have done that easily. It would just have been common courtesy. But that meeting was the last time I spoke to two of the people in that room, Norman Crighton and Graham Wallace.

Rangers put out an official club statement on their website that said Ibrox was "sacrosanct". But the year before Rangers had put out an official club statement on their website which said Sons of

Struth were encouraging supporters to commit unruly behaviour. I don't think anybody believed a word of anything they said. I certainly didn't.

I must admit it affected me terribly. I went from the euphoria of thinking we had achieved something that we were all working towards to the realisation that nothing was going to happen. I had hardly slept on the Wednesday night. I was like a kid on Christmas Eve waiting for Santa to come. I thought: "We've done this! We've secured Ibrox for the Rangers fans! I can't wait until tomorrow! I'm so proud!"

I was in a bad place personally at the time. I had just split up from a three year relationship and I was back home living with my parents. My business was also suffering badly because of the amount of time I was devoting to Sons of Struth. I was in a fairly fragile state as it was. But that really left me reeling. The next week was just a blur. It wasn't pleasant. I was definitely depressed.

Picking myself up from that was arduous. I did keep going. But it took a bit of time to regroup and get, as our legendary manager Jock Wallace would say, the battle fever on again. When we did eventually renew our campaign there was no going back to the board. We had opened the door to them and they had stuck two fingers up at us.

Only 19,000 fans bought seasons tickets by deadline day. They eventually got it up to around 21,000. I think the majority of people didn't renew because they didn't like the board. The quality of football the side was playing, the level the team was performing at and the standard of opposition will all have come into people's thinking too.

All that the season ticket boycott did was bring the need to borrow money forward. If all 36,000 fans had renewed their books, at an increased price on the previous season, Rangers still wouldn't have had enough money to see out the campaign. Simple back-of-a-fag-packet accountancy showed that.

We asked people to boycott season tickets and to boycott a one-off League Cup game against St. Johnstone. When you put your head above the parapet like that you have to accept you are going to get some flak and prepare for it. But some folk said: "You're going to destroy the club!" Why? We were going to run out of money anyway.

I can't believe they were naive and stupid enough to have their minds changed. When I had my meeting with Graham Wallace in February I asked him if he was being worked from the back. He assured me he was his own man. But if anybody wanted proof that the directors of the club didn't actually hold any power that was it.

It reminded me of selling a bloke a car. You show him all of the vehicle's best features, take him for a test drive, offer him a payment plan and he agrees to buy it. Then he comes in the next day and tells you: "The wife's said: 'No!'"

It was later suggested to me that we had agreed not to speak about the meeting and reneged on that much to the annoyance of the board. But that was drivel. We were asked to keep the meeting secret beforehand and we did so. It was kept out of the newspapers and off social media. Then we were asked at the meeting if we wanted to keep what was discussed confidential. We explained that we couldn't do that because we were representing thousands of Rangers fans and we needed to inform them what had been discussed.

That was around the time that Paul Tyrrell, the former Head of Communications at Manchester City, Everton and Liverpool, was brought in as a media advisor to Graham. I Googled his name and immediately found he had compared certain sections of the Liverpool support to the Khmer Rouge during his time at Anfield.

I thought: "This guy's going to love me! Khmer Rouge? I wonder who he'll compare Sons of Struth to." But within hours of putting that online I had been contacted by a Liverpool supporter who said: "Paul's actually alright."

Paul and I certainly agreed on a lot of things about Rangers during his time at Ibrox. But he was adamant that releasing our statement on the night of our meeting was the wrong thing to do. I think though, that is only because he had been told by the people in that meeting that we had all agreed not to divulge what was said. That wasn't the case.

We were asked the question: "Is this meeting going to be kept under wraps?" We all said: "No, it isn't." If they had asked us to keep it silent for a day then I'm sure we all would have agreed. But we didn't. I have spoken to Paul at length about this. For the life of me, I still can't understand what the issue was.

We all suspected – along with every journalist in Scotland - that Jack Irvine was still working for Sandy Easdale. But reporters couldn't print it and lose a source of stories.

At the end of that meeting at Ibrox we got asked: "Is there any other business?" Pointing at Sandy Easdale, I said: "Aye, he's still being represented by Jack Irvine." Sandy said: "No I'm no'!' I said: "Sandy, I've got an email that went from Jack Irvine to you to your lawyer to me!" They had inadvertently forgotten to delete what was underneath the message when they forwarded it to me.

In June he released a statement which read: "I wish to confirm that neither Media House International Ltd nor its Executive Chairman Jack Irvine acts for me or any of my associated companies. Mr Irvine and I severed our business relationship on August 23, 2013, when Mr Irvine renewed his contract with Rangers Football Club. It is therefore wholly untrue to suggest or imply that Mr Irvine and I have a business relationship.".

In August when James and Sandy Easdale were reported to be interested in buying the Ferguson Shipyard in Port Glasgow after it had been put into administration there was footage of them on Reporting Scotland that night inspecting the site. Standing there alongside them, as bold as brass, was Jack Irvine. Maybe he had just chummed along as a pal.

I don't think Graham Wallace was a bad person. He made mistakes and at times I think he was naive. He was born and brought up in Dumfries. He didn't come from the back streets of Glasgow. The guys he was up against did. They played dirty, he played it by the book.

I honestly don't know how many people pledged their support to Ibrox 1972. I didn't want to know. If it had been two people I would have been downhearted. It would also have scuppered what we were trying to achieve. If it had been 20,000 then I would have been cock-a-hoop and there would have been a danger I wouldn't have been so driven pursuing our goal. I deliberately didn't try to find out. To this day, I genuinely don't know if the number was in single figures or tens of thousands.

CHAPTER 12
BOMBER ON BOARD

"Every single one of them knows who Sons of Struth are and they're right behind you."

John Brown, Rangers great.

AFTER the final home game of the 2013/14 season against Stranraer, after the supporters had paid tribute to Sandy Jardine and after we had been presented with the SPFL League One trophy, I stood at my seat for a moment of quiet reflection. I thought to myself: "I might not be here again." I had sat there for 32 years, including with my late grandparents, so it was quite emotional and upsetting.

I looked around the section as I did so and I noticed a handful of other people doing exactly the same thing. Some of them came over to me, shook my hand and gave me messages of support. People I had sat with for years and years and had never spoken to. I think most people's opinion was: "I would rather put one seat at risk than 52,000."

In the run-up to our meeting with the board, I had travelled to supporters clubs across the country. I had answered their questions and told them all the same thing. I had said: "If you support what we are doing then stand beside us. If you don't agree with what we're doing then please hold off buying your season ticket for as long as you can. The public can't buy your ticket until after the renewal date."

I had people come up to me in tears and tell me they couldn't give up their seat because it was their father's dying wish they keep it going. I told them: You know what? Go and renew your season ticket!" How could I ask them not to in those circumstances?

I had parents with disabled children come up and tell me:"We've waited a long time to get this spot?" I know that getting those kind of seats isn't an easy thing at any football club never mind one the size of Rangers. I told them:"Fine. You batter in. Go and renew your season tickets."

There were lots of different reasons – and some excuses – for renewing. We didn't have a problem with any of them. But we asked people to show solidarity with their fellow supporters by holding off doing so. I assured people:"Even if you renew after the Friday deadline you'll still get your old seat back."

We knew how the ticket office worked. It was going to take them two or three days to get through all of the renewals. Only after that could they start allocating seats to new applicants. We knew there were thousands, possibly tens of thousands, who were going to renew, but who were holding off.

I don't think anybody disagreed with us. Not really. Securing Ibrox could only possibly be a good thing for Rangers. What football fan could possibly take issue with safeguarding the future of their club's stadium? Some people may have had issues with how we were going about it. But nobody could say it wasn't a worthwhile exercise.

I was impressed by the number of people who refused to renew. Around half of the season ticket holders withheld their money. It was quite a gesture. It was a far harder thing for them to do than hold a card up during a protest at a game.

I felt the people were in charge were far more dangerous if we gave them a large sum of money than small sums of money throughout the season. By attending on a game-by-game basis – as we were urging fans to do - we were actually giving them slightly more money. But a business doesn't want peaks and troughs in income.

The slogans we came up with were "GAME BY GAME OR GET MORE OF THE SAME" and "SUPPORT THE TEAM NOT THE REGIME". We didn't actually urge people to completely boycott football matches. That was the ultimate sacrifice and only came much later on. All we were asking for were assurances over Ibrox. That was not a big ask in our eyes.

The advantage of drip-feeding them cash was highlighted towards the end of their time when we were able to completely remove their financial support. It gave the supporters real control and power.

People – the same folk who claimed I was being bankrolled by Dave King - have suggested the plan all along was to starve the board out. That, though, just wasn't the case.

People within our own fanbase ridiculed us. They would say: "Why are you asking for something the club has already agreed to?" But they hadn't. They had issued meaningless statements to the AIM Stock Exchange and on their official website. Those missives included phrases like "at this time we have no desire to use Ibrox as security".

But there had been so many board changes over the previous couple of years. We wanted something far more concrete. Not from individuals either from the club. We even suggested they just give us a guarantee for the 2014/15 season. We didn't want something cast in stone for eternity.

It would have given us 12 months to study how we could safeguard the ground properly. We could have examined doing something similar to the Chelsea Pitch Owners for example. We could have created a trust with a membership scheme. Not only would that have secured that stadium for future generations of supporters it could also have brought income into the club. If done properly, it could have saved the club money. There are lots of government initiatives which could have been explored.

A lot of the fans who had been instrumental in our campaign felt we should take the summer off. But I believed it was important to remain in the public eye as a reminder the club had refused the fans what we believed was a reasonable request. When you think you have won and somebody cheats you my natural reaction was to respond to that. So I launched an online petition, arranged a postcard protest and organised a march to Ibrox in July.

I didn't want to give the board a minute's rest. I didn't want apathy to set in. If we had taken a break I have no doubt more fans would have renewed their season tickets. I felt we had to keep the fight alive during the summer. People said: "Just give it a rest!"

I told them: "No, I won't give it a bloody rest! This is my football club we're fighting for here." I couldn't do it. They would have got a rest if they had done what they said they were going to do and given us written assurances about the stadium. I decided to give it to them stinking that summer.

We got postcards printed up. They had a space for a name followed by the line "will buy a season ticket if any of the following happen". Then we had boxes for them to tick next to statements like "the board is removed" or "Ibrox is secured for the supporters". It was just driving home the message: "We want to renew our season tickets – but we want something in return."

In May around 500 fans stuck postcards through the door at Ibrox. We gathered in Mafeking Street just adjacent to the Louden Tavern, marched behind the Copland Road Stand, in front of the Main Stand and then past the back of the Broomloan Road Stand, past the ticket office on to the front door of Argyle House. Oddly enough, the front door doesn't have a letterbox.

But we got some good photographs. We got everyone to line up at the ticket office and gave them red cards to add a visual element to what we were doing. The line stretched half the length of the stadium. It showed how many people wanted to buy them but weren't. A quote we gave to the media was: "This is the biggest queue we've had at the ticket office all summer!" We got on the front pages as well as the back pages of the papers which was what we wanted.

But the biggest event we did over the close season was the March on Ibrox. There was a Free Palestine march from Glasgow city centre to the BBC studios at Pacific Quay that same day which created an issue. It was attended by a lot of Celtic supporters and specifically the ultra element of the Parkhead club's fan base. The police were concerned about the close proximity of that event to ours.

There was a lot of planning involved in that march. It probably required the most preparation of anything I did throughout the whole campaign. It was certainly the most pressure I was under. I started preparing for it in May after we failed to get the assurances we were looking for over the stadium. From a personal point of view, I had to do something.

I couldn't let them away with that. I don't like bullies. I don't like liars. As far as I could see, they were both. I thought: "How can I get back at them? How can I encourage fans to get involved?" The idea of walking to Kinning Park, where our previous stadium was situated, to Ibrox was quite symbolic. We also decided it would get underway at three o'clock on a Saturday afternoon when obviously most of our games kicked off.

Because we were going on the road I had to go through Glasgow City Council and meet with their officials three times. They asked me what numbers I was expecting. I estimated between 2,000 and 3,000 would turn up. One of the stipulations, which I was unaware of, was that we needed a one in ten ratio for marshalls to marchers. We required between 200 and 300 stewards in high-visibility jackets. I was asked to have those helpers with previous experience working closely with those without experience.

An interesting thing happened. To generate support, I opened a page on the website I had created to give us a greater online presence, www.sonsofstruth.co.uk. I wanted us to look more professional. We had the accusation flung at us that we were nothing more than a Facebook page. I thought: "Well, if it makes a difference to people, I'll set up a website." I had no experience of that sort of thing, but I did it myself.

The page on the website asked for volunteers. If you filled in a form it automatically converted that into an email which was forwarded to me. I just counted up the number of replies I got in my inbox to determine how many people would assist me. Very quickly, I got over 100. Before long, I stopped looking. I thought: "We'll get enough marshalls easily."

One night before a meeting with the council I went into my email account to access the information so I could put it on a spreadsheet. When I opened it up I only had seven emails. Somebody had hacked in and corrupted all of the data we had amassed. It was the week of the march. I had to go in the next day and wing it.

One of my biggest selling points was the number of marshalls I had. But I only had the names of around half a dozen. They asked me: "Are you going to have enough marshalls?" I told them: "No problem whatsoever." I appealed for marshalls on our Facebook page in the lead-up to the march and kept my fingers crossed enough of them would turn up.

Sandy Chugg would disappear from time to time to deal with the personal issues he had on his plate. Then, out of the blue, he would just turn up again. He was back on the scene and realised something wasn't right. I had to tell him what happened. He told me:"Don't worry about it for another minute. You've got enough to deal with. I'll get marshalls."

Sandy had been involved in the march to Hampden after Rangers had gone into administration in 2012 and had got to know a lot of boys who had helped with that. We were also able to tap into many members of the Orange Order who do a lot of marching and know about that side of things.

Sandy took total control. If only 100 or so had turned up the police would have called it off. Fortunately, between 200 and 300 trapped.

The council only, as their protocols required, gave me the go-ahead the day before. The piece of paper saying I had the all clear only arrived on the Friday and the march was on the Saturday. It was weird. I like to have a date and work to it. But it was only rubber stamped at the very last minute.

On the day of the march it rained all morning. It was a torrential downpour. It turned out to be the only wet day in the whole of July. It was a monsoon. When I turned up a couple of hours before it was due to start in order to get organised and saw the weather I thought to myself:"This just ain't gonna happen today. We're going to get 500 people if we're lucky."

Those taking part were congregating at a triangle of pubs on Paisley Road West, The Bellrock, The District Bar and The Grapes. I kept nipping along to see how many folk there were there. I was telling myself:"This is going to be embarrassing."Then, just 10 minutes before we were due to start, I had to go speak to the police officer in charge to go through a list of questions for legal reasons.

Because of the weather, we went and sat in a police mini-bus. The rain was getting heavier and heavier. I was looking out and thinking:"We've got more marshalls than marchers!"

Andy Smillie had given us the use of a flatbed truck for the day. He had put scaffolding around the side and hung up flags. Before we set off, John Brown, the former Rangers player, Ian McColl, from the Founders Trail, Sandy Chugg and I were going to stand on it and speak. I convinced myself there was going to be virtually nobody to address.

But as I got up onto the truck something happened. People started to empty out of pubs. They popped out from behind trees. They emerged from closes. They got out of cars parked up sidestreets. I can remember looking around at this and thinking: "We've pulled it off again! In the pissing rain as well! They've got what we're trying to do." It turned out to be quite an inspiring day.

When you're a football fan, you disappear from your wife, your husband, your kids, your boyfriend, your girlfriend, your family, for hours on end every Saturday for 10 months a year. So in the summer you tend to do things with them again. You go shopping, go on holiday, go on days out. There were a lot of reasons for people not to turn up. But they came in their droves.

The speeches took around 10 minutes. Ian spoke about the history of the club and the significance of the route. The Founding Fathers had played in and rented stadiums for 14 nomadic years. But during that time they had always wanted their own home. They worked tirelessly to make the move from Kinning Park to Ibrox. We were making the same journey in an attempt to secure what they had striven for some 120 years before. We were trying to achieve the same thing in some respects.

Accusing a football club board of being liars and bad people is quite confrontational. It is difficult to get former players to stand alongside you when you are saying that. But trying to safeguard your stadium is easier. We had support from John, Lorenzo Amoruso, Michael Mols, Marco Negri, Nacho Novo, Alex Rae and Bobby Russell. They all got involved.

We fed comments and stories from the former players to the media in the week leading up to the march. For example, we put out photos of Michael along with quotes from him about why he thought our event was a worthwhile idea. Punters buy into that and it definitely helped us to attract good numbers a lot.

I first met Alex at the start of that year not long after he had left his job as assistant manager to Paul Ince at Blackpool. He came along to one of the planning meetings at the Ivory Hotel. Afterwards he told us he was shocked at what he had heard and grateful that we were standing up against the board.

Alex didn't return to coaching until the start of the following season when he became assistant to the former Rangers manager Alex McLeish at KRC Genk in Belgium. He spent most of the intervening period working as a pundit with Radio Clyde. He would get asked a lot of questions about Rangers on the phone-in and would often call me so he could give informed answers on the subjects he was being asked about.

His calls didn't stop when he moved to Genk. He got in touch just to find out what was happening to his beloved football club back in Glasgow. We spoke about a lot of other things too. He was a long way from his family and had a great deal of spare time on his hands in the evening. As a youth coach, it was fantastic for me to talk to somebody so knowledgeable about the game and tactics.

One day he got in touch to ask why I had phoned him at two o'clock the previous morning. I had no idea. I couldn't remember ringing him. I had been out on the town and only had a vague recollection of the previous evening due the amount of alcohol I had imbibed. Then I remembered. I had bumped into a group of Millwall supporters. One of them, a great lad called Spanish Joe, hold told me Alex Rae was his all-time favourite player. So I called him so he could chat to his hero.

Alex was obviously fast asleep. But soon after that Spanish Joe managed get in touch with him. He was really appreciative and offered to look after me if I was ever down in London and take me to a game at The Den. Joe had been a bit of a lad in his younger years. But he had turned his life around. When I met him he was working in his local community and trying to prevent kids from making the same poor choices and mistakes he had.

Spanish Joe was fascinated by Sons of Struth. He seemed amazed that a football fan had taken on such a challenge. He said: "You're not the first person I've met who has fought for their club, but you're the first who hasn't done their fighting on the terraces." He was just one of the many interesting characters I met throughout this whole process.

I met Alex McLeish at the Rangers Supporters Trust annual dinner shortly after that. I was introduced to him as "the guy Sandy Easdale sued". He bumped into me as he was leaving and stood talking for a good half an hour about what was happening at Ibrox. He said he had heard rumours and stories when he had been working down in England and admitted he had dismissed them as being too far-fetched. As I confirmed they weren't he grew more and more concerned.

Marco Negri contacted me on Facebook one day out of the blue. I was convinced it was a fake account. The Italian was probably the most enigmatic player Rangers have had in my lifetime - and we have had a few of them.

He scored five goals on his league debut against Dundee United at Ibrox in 1997 and 33 in total by the turn of the year. That was more than the entire Hearts team had netted by that stage in the season. But he sustained an eye injury after that and hardly played again. Rangers ended up just failing to win a record tenth league title in a row on the final day of the season and he disappeared as quickly as he had arrived.

But we had a short online chat and then a telephone call. I convinced myself he was no imposter, gave him more details of our march and he agreed to promote it in the media. I have spoken to Marco a number of times since and met him on a couple of occasions. He has altered the opinions of a fair few supporters who were disillusioned at how his time at Ibrox ended with his support for our cause.

Michael Mols was another former striker and huge hero of mine who asked supporters to join in with our march. I didn't realise how close Michael was with Marco until I popped along to a book signing session the latter was doing in Glasgow one day that summer. The two of them were both there together.

The Rangers Supporters Trust dinner was that evening, but, because of my impoverished financial situation at the time, I was unable to afford tickets. I was disappointed as Gillian, the lassie I had started seeing by then, enjoyed them and I wanted to treat her for all of the support she had given me during the tough times I had been through.

Robert Marshall of the Louden Tavern Ibrox had been in touch and asked if I would come along to speak to the Lewis and Harris Rangers Supporters Club who were having their annual event in his establishment. I agreed to pop along for an hour or two.

But then I got a text from Gordon Dinnie of the Rangers Supporters Trust asking if I would be able to arrange some former players to come to a table which they had set aside for them due to some late cancellations. I started texting people straight away and within hours I had lined up Michael, Marco and John MacDonald.

I sat next to Michael and spent the whole meal talking about youth football and our plans for a Sons of Struth Football Academy. I told him that I hoped to raise enough money to make it a Coerver partner club.

Wiel Coerver was a Dutch football manager who was dubbed the "Albert Einstein of football" after devising the Coerver Method of coaching. Michael had been Coerver coached himself as a boy and spent an hour showing me Coerver drills using salt and pepper pots to illustrate the techniques used. It was a fantastic evening. And it just got better.

Chris Graham and I nipped away after the meal to honour our agreement with Robert at the Louden. When we got there one of the Lewis and Harris committee men told us that the fan ownership scheme Rangers First, the Rangers Supporters Trust and Sons of Struth had been awarded their Player of the Year awards for all we had done for the club. Chris, Ricki Neill and I each received a beautifully engraved hip flask and an official club tie. It was very humbling.

Bomber spoke before the march and then I got up and said some words. I was really inspired by what I saw in front of me. I was moved by so many people coming out in such terrible conditions to show their support for what we were trying to achieve.

I said to them:"I promise you we are going to win this. The reason for that is we are Rangers supporters. We were here before them and we'll be here after them. We will outlive any board. I don't know if we'll win in a month, a year or 10 years. But as long as we keep at it we will win."

Then off we went. We marched from halfway down Scotland

Street where the old stadium used to be, passed the subway station and turned left onto Paisley Road West. I was at the front and as we got a few hundred yards further along a policeman said to me: "Craig, you've pulled some crowd. Go and have a look. They're still coming around the corner." I went and stood on the pavement. All I could see was a sea of people. More people were coming out of pubs, cafes, shops and cars and joining in.

One guy came all the way from Hong Kong. He didn't come over to Scotland specifically to take part in the march. But he was delighted when he found out it was on just after his plane landed in Glasgow. So he came along and joined in.

There were elderly people with walking aids. There were families with dogs. There were babies who were just months old being pushed in prams. There were banners, flags, whistles, all sorts of things. It was a touching show of power and strength and unity.

When we got to Edmiston Drive we turned right towards Ibrox. I was able to look back once again in amazement to see how many people there were. When we got to the front door of the stadium the truck was parked and waiting – the police had shut down the whole street just like they do on match days - and we got up on it again. It must have taken 15 minutes for everyone to arrive. The police later said around 3,500 took part.

Somebody filmed the march out of one of the high rise flats near the ground. I am led to believe he did so to show us up, to highlight how few people had supported us, to have a pop at us for not representing the majority of supporters. He put it up on YouTube. But all it showed was a condensed crowd of several thousand people. It was one of the best bits of publicity we had. Apparently he was a Rangers fan who thought we were idiots. He posted a message on our Facebook page. He asked: "Why are you trying to protect Ibrox? It will never be in any danger." Unfortunately, we were proved right in time.

There were some people inside the stadium looking out to see what we were doing. But they were probably as enthusiastic as we were. The messages of support I have received from employees from the day we started up have been phenomenal.

Wee Nacho Novo had, unbeknown to me, joined us on the route.

He got up on the truck when we got to the stadium and said a few words along with John, Sandy and I. I can still remember what I told them. I said:"Seeing so many you here as I stand next to John and Nacho, two of my heroes, makes me so proud. I don't think I could be any prouder if I played 10 minutes on the park."

There hadn't been any discussions about the march. I pulled together a meeting one day. Around half a dozen of us turned up and I could tell instantly there was no energy or enthusiasm for it. I think the feeling was:"It's the summer. Can we no' just gie it a break for a bit?" I asked a few people to carry out tasks and nobody came back to me. So I did it myself. It was just billed as "A March to Ibrox". It was designed to save the stadium. But it didn't achieve anything.

But the march was a success. It showed the strength of feeling there was among the support. It highlighted the displeasure there was. We got some great publicity too. It made the newspapers, radio and television. One thing I have learned throughout this whole experience is that journalists need to write stories. If you are a sports journalist and no sport is being played then you are scraping around for stories. I wasn't unaware of that fact. It was easy to sell it to the papers. It probably got so much coverage because there was nothing else for them to write about.

When you are a rank and file fan, you tend to think a certain journalist or a particular media outlet is pro-Celtic or anti-Rangers. But I soon discovered they needed to write a story regardless of their allegiance. If a story lands in their lap, good or bad, about Rangers then they will publish it. If you can give them something then, as long as nothing major is breaking at the same time, then you will get your story out there.

I couldn't understand why the people responsible for Rangers PR didn't understand this. I got up to speed with it pretty quickly. If I wanted to get something into the paper I would plan when to do it. I didn't put anything out on a Monday because they are writing about that weekend's games. On a Friday they are previewing the weekend's games. So you want to get your message out there on a Tuesday or a Wednesday.

If you knew something else was on which may have impacted on the showing you would get you delayed. We got caught out on very few occasions. What we did was only overshadowed by something else once or twice at the most. I thought: "Why don't the club just do what we're doing?" They were paying hundreds of thousands of pounds a year to a multitude of faceless advisors and expensive agencies. But the club was getting an absolute kicking online and in the papers every day.

Most of the stuff they fed the media actually benefitted our campaign, not them as a club. I used to scratch my head and say: "Why are you paying this guy?" I told Sandy Easdale that about Jack Irvine in a meeting once. I said: "I could do a better job than this guy!" I offered to repair his reputation. He spoke to his PR man who knocked it back.

When Graham Wallace appointed Paul Tyrrell as his media advisor, I spoke to him on the phone. He asked me: "Who does your publicity? Who puts out your press releases? Who's responsible for your Twitter output? Who updates your Facebook page?" I said: "Me. Me. Me. Me." He said: "Are you having a laugh? What sort of public relations background have you got?" I said: "None." He didn't believe me. He genuinely thought we employed a team of people, PR executives, IT specialists and the like, to advise us. Now, maybe he was just blowing smoke up my backside. But I sensed he was being genuine.

He said: "But you made a video for an alternative strip you were launching! Who did that?" I said: "Me." He said: "You're like a one man army! The exposure you're getting for one man is ridiculous! You should be doing my job." I have no qualifications or professional expertise on that front. But, I tell you what, I got bloody good results. We got more in the paper than the club did.

When the Union of Fans formed and we were issuing statements we were driving the agenda. We controlled what went in the papers. They were easy to deal with. If the club banned them, as they did with the Daily Record, it just made our lives even easier.

The majority of stunts we pulled were designed to get our message across to a wider audience. We needed to use the media to do that. Our Facebook page could get 150,000 hits a week. But a newspaper can attract that sort of online traffic in a day. We had to use them to get our message across. Not all Rangers fans go online. In fact, I am pretty sure you would struggle to fill an enclosure at Ibrox with them.

When Rangers First, the fan ownership scheme, was in its infancy, John Brown turned up at one of the meetings we held in The Louden Tavern, Ibrox. He listened and made a few points. After it had finished I went over and introduced myself. I asked him if he could help us in any way. I must have asked around a hundred former players to help. They all came up with various excuses about how they couldn't get involved.

To be fair to Bomber, he gave me a genuine reason. He said:"Look, I've just lost my job as Dundee manager. From my first day at Dens Park, people were asking: 'Why's he so involved in what's going on at Rangers?' I lost a job at Rangers at the start of this thing for opening my mouth. I can't afford it to cost me another job. I have to work and bring in money like anybody else."

It obviously wasn't the answer I wanted, but I thanked him for his honesty. Like most Rangers fans, I felt he had done his bit. I had nothing but admiration and respect for him and that didn't change one bit with his response. But a few months later I was contacted by a mutual friend and told:"Bomber's up for the fight now." I called him and he told me he was prepared do anything which needed to be done to win the fight. I think the Blue Nose in him came to the fore. He had just had enough like the rest of us.

The first thing he helped us with was the petition. We got 8,000 signatures on our Save Ibrox campaign. We spent a few hundred pounds getting it bound professionally. It looked like a phone book when we had finished with it.

The best way to describe John is to say he is as passionate about Rangers as any fan who sits in the stands or stands on a terrace watching the team. He is just fortunate that he got the chance to fulfil his dream and play for his heroes. But that hasn't changed how he acts or thinks about the club.

We met outside Argyle House at Ibrox when we were going to hand in the petition. When we arrived, the photographers asked us to go around to the iconic blue gates to pose for pictures. As we walked around we talked. It was the first time I had chatted to him at any length. He had just come back from a legends' tournament in Hong Kong. He stated rhyming off the names of all the players who had been involved.

He said: "Do you know something? Every single one of them knows what you're doing. They know who Craig Houston is, who Sons of Struth are and they're right behind you." I was gobsmacked to think guys I had cheered on at the football knew who I was. I said: "I don't know how to take that? It's fantastic these guys know what's happening, but the flipside of that is this. Where are they?' The guys he mentioned, though, did come to the fore after that and help us in a variety of different ways.

I filled all of the necessary information in on the epetition. What do we want to achieve? That sort of stuff. The last section was titled "recipients". You could input the email addresses you wanted the signatures to go to. So I put in Sandy Easdale's and Graham Wallace's official club accounts.

A few months before that, Jack Irvine had sent Sandy Easdale – despite the fact he wasn't, according to Sandy anyway, representing him any more - an email pointing out something on the Sons of Struth Facebook page he didn't like with a catty comment. Sandy had then forwarded it to his lawyer who in turn forwarded it to me. It had his work email address at McGill's Buses on it. So I put that in the petition too.

I sat up in the early hours of a Monday morning publicising the petition on Facebook, Twitter and some supporters forums to make sure people knew about it and signed up for it. I made it known that every time somebody signed it and wrote a comment it would be forwarded to Sandy Easdale and Graham Wallace. That helped to encourage people.

By the time I went to my bed there were a couple of hundred signatures. When I got up there were over 1,500. I burst out laughing. I thought: "They're going to go into their work first thing on Monday morning and there'll be 1,500 emails waiting for them from Rangers fans saying they're not happy and demanding legal guarantees over Ibrox."

I received a few emails from Sandy Easdale's lawyer Peter Watson that day. He said I shouldn't have his private email address and demanded to know how I had obtained it. I replied: "You gave it to me!" They were trying to get me by whatever means possible at that time. There was definitely a witch hunt going on. But my defence was sound. They told me to take it off. I just ignored them. I thought: "Och, sod them!"

Change.org do thousands of these petitions. People petition against governments, banks and multinational companies. If there was a problem with putting an email address in it would have arisen long before I came along. It was just another example of Sandy Easdale/ Jack Irvine/Peter Watson attempting to block our activities. I felt they tried to determine what the law was sometimes.

When you start being threatened by lawyers it is a worry. But when somebody tries to sue you for £200,000 and you come through it unscathed your attitude changes. You then decide to fight it. Hardly any of the hundreds of strongly-worded emails and letters that lawyers send out become actual actions. It is just intimidation. At one stage, I received correspondence from the lawyer's lawyer telling me he was going to sue me. That is how ridiculous it became.

I learned quite quickly that every time a lawyer sent an email to me he sent an invoice to somebody else. So I would have email conversations with him. I asked him lots of questions. I would say something like: "Can you please clarify who you are representing in this instance?" That would generate another email. On and on it went. One email became a dozen. It became a game to me. By doing that, I hoped whoever was shelling out would say at some stage: "Hold on a minute here!" As I suspected, they backed down over the petition. Nobody could see his email address. I hadn't published it. They claimed it was harassment. But they had given it to me.

CHAPTER 13
FLASH MOB

"I have not had any dealings with Rafat Rizvi."

Sandy Easdale, Rangers shareholder.

WHEN the 2014/15 season got underway, many of the fans who had refused to buy season tickets started attending on a game-by-game basis. A lot stayed away altogether and attendances soon started to drop dramatically.

I personally went to every home match, and the vast majority of away ones, to begin with. I would go in to Bar '72 in the Sandy Jardine Stand, the Copland Road Stand or the Broomloan Road Stand for games at Ibrox.

Sandy Chugg and I went and sat with the Blue Order and the Union Bears in the Broomloan Road Stand a couple of times. Both organisations had been such a great help to us throughout our campaign so we returned the favour by supporting their displays. I must say I quite enjoyed the experience.

They are great lads. Most of them are in their teens and their early twenties. But they certainly know about the history and traditions of the club. Some of the older fans do get exasperated with their conduct. But I think they will be the reason the stories about our club are carried from one generation to the next. To a man, for example, they will all be able to name the members of the 1972 European Cup Winners' Cup team.

I hadn't appreciated the time and effort which went into their banners and flags before I went and sat with them. We joined the Union Bears for the game at Ibrox immediately before the Scottish independence referendum in September. They had a huge union flag and a saltire with "VOTE NO" written along the bottom of it. It covered the entire section. As we were standing under the display, I turned to Sandy and said: "I reckon we're the only ones here old enough to vote!"

A couple of Sons of Struth supporters, Brian Bowman and Les Henderson, took over from me behind the directors' box. They kept the heat up on the board at matches by holding up banners as they came in and out. We, meanwhile, waited for the next issue to arise so we could get in amongst them again.

When Rangers announced they were forming an official fans board we asked ourselves: "Are we better fighting from the outside or the inside?" There was a bit of talk about putting members of Sons of Struth or the Union of Fans up for election. In the end we decided against it. The feeling was it would be a board controlled by the board.

There were a couple of people on it when it was first formed who we knew. For example, Billy Paterson represented the disabled fans. We championed him on social media when he put himself up for election. He had already used his knowledge and power as a shareholder to force the club to make the directors' pay structures public. We felt somebody like that would be good to have involved.

But the rest of the 12 were unknown to us. We had heard of some of them. Others we knew for a fact were pro-board. In the end, it only lasted around four months and those involved did a fantastic job. They ended up giving the old regime a vote of no confidence. By the time they were dissolved three of their members had joined the Sons of Struth.

It was obvious the club was trying to disassociate itself from the existing, and in many cases long-standing, fans groups. So I set up a Sons of Struth membership scheme. I thought: "If they can see we represent and talk for thousands of people it will help us going forward. After all, they talk to people who run a supporters' bus which has 50 fans on." Before long, we had thousands of members.

Sandy and I also devised a plan to set up a Sons of Struth youth football club. I spoke to the two fans who had designed a red and black shirt to raise funds for a charitable cause about how to market it and use suppliers. We planned to do something similar.

We even went so far as getting samples made, drawing up some adverts and lining up two former players for a promotional video. I asked different people at the club how to go about it. They refused to speak to me. I then got a phone call one day telling me if I proceeded with it I would get taken to the court and sued for "passing off".

That, coupled with those people who were alleging online that I was a spiv and was going to make a lot of money out of my campaign against those in charge of the club, made me decide it wasn't worth pursuing. At that time, there were bigger battles to fight. But it was disappointing. We could have got a Sons of Struth Youth Academy up and running far earlier and Rangers Youth Development could have benefitted hugely.

The Rangers Supporters Trust got wind of it and turned it into an alternative shirt which was sold to raise money to buy shares. Red and black are the iconic colours of the traditional Rangers socks as well as of the Burgh of Govan. It has been phenomenally successful and has, to date, raised over £60,000.

IN August I was informed by a source within the club that Charles Green had sold the naming rights to Ibrox to Mike Ashley for £1 during his stint as chief executive. At the time, I wasn't sure it was accurate. Throughout our campaign, I was told dozens of things which had taken place. I wasn't daft. I knew that sometimes the information I was being fed was false. People wanted me to make inaccurate accusations so they could then discredit me.

When I received this particular nugget of information I was instantly wary. The individual who told me was extremely reliable and I was convinced it was accurate. But I did think: "Am I getting set up to take a fall here?" So I didn't immediately rush to my laptop and put it up on the Sons of Struth Facebook page. I spoke to a handful of people about it in an attempt to get it verified.

Before I knew it, I received a phone call from Keith Jackson of the Daily Record about it. It was on the front and the back page of his newspaper the next day. But I was quite happy for them to run it. The bigger the story the better it was to put it out in the media. It definitely had more of an impact that way than by putting it online. Creating a stir was always more important to me than breaking a story myself.

It became apparent to a lot of people involved in the campaign that I was receiving information from inside the club which they weren't privy to. I was asked at a meeting of the Union of Fans one day if I would share everything I was told with them going forward. My answer was: "Categorically, no." But there was no ill feeling as a result.

In the first weekend of September we decided to have a jolly boys outing to Blackpool. I had been in contact with a supporter called Mark Campbell online for several months. He and a few other members of the Blackpool True Blues had clubbed together and opened The Gallant Pioneer Rangers pub. We decided to head down and show support for their new venture.

About a dozen of us left on a mini bus driven by Sie Leslie. It was to be a busy day for Sie. He conducted the question and answer session which Sandy Chugg and I gave the regulars and put on the disco. It was a well-attended event. A lot of fans travelled from Scotland and from all across England.

I personally thought the first half of the Q&A went really well. Sandy and I had answered questions from the supporters and tried to enlighten them about issues which we had an insight into or events we had been involved in. We nipped out for a break and a cigarette feeling it was all going swimmingly.

Then we heard big George address the crowd inside. He said: "If any of you filmed that or repeat a word of anything that those two have said on social media then you'll have me to answer to!"

When he came out to join us shortly afterwards I asked him: "What's up?"

He replied: "Have you no idea what you and your daft pal were saying up there? You were doing alright until you started to say what you felt about certain directors. You've been on the drink for 12 hours solid! I'm surprised the pair of you are still standing!"

The crowd must have either been firmly in agreement with us or petrified of George. Whatever the reason was, nothing appeared on the internet. We left with more Sons of Struth supporters than we had arrived with. The trip was a great success.

THERE was a split appearing in the actual Rangers board by that time. We got wind of it and started to highlight it on Facebook and Twitter. To begin with, the divide between the directors wasn't actually that great. But I could tell by the way statements were being released and information was being leaked to the media what was happening.

The Rangers board had tried to divide and conquer the fans before that. They had published lies about our activities on their official website and in newspaper interviews, had fed misinformation to bloggers to put out into the public domain and had infiltrated social media with made-up posters purporting to be supporters who backed them and were against us.

So I decided to do the same thing. I exaggerated the differences of opinion about the direction the club should take which were developing. But I was certainly hearing from reliable sources that relations weren't as cordial as they should have been between those who were running the club at that time.

Phillip Nash, the financial consultant who had been made a director in July of 2014, and Graham Wallace, the chief executive who had brought him in, were on one side. James Easdale, the non-executive director, and David Somers, the chairman, were on the other.

Then you had Norman Crighton. Initially he sided more with Easdale and Somers. But we received word he was swithering. In the end, he swung the other way. Crighton, Nash and Wallace decided the best move for Rangers was to accept an offer of investment from the group which Dave King was fronting.

They were only interested in what was right, not the characters. If Mike Ashley had decided to invest in the club instead of putting in loans then I am sure they would have backed him. It just so happened that it was Dave King and then The Three Bears consortium who did that. It was clearly the right thing to do so they supported him.

There were people inside the club doing things for the right reasons and people inside the club doing things for their own reasons. I believe that Nash and Wallace did things for the betterment of the club. Sandy Easdale kept trying to tell everyone he was only doing what was best. But if you are in a room when a bank robbery is being planned then you are, for me, as guilty as those who carried it out.

The way I saw it, Wallace was in there working away for the good of Rangers while Easdale was in there to represent the interests of those shareholders who had given him their proxy and to protect his own position. If Dave King was allowed to come in it would have diluted their stake and resulted in him losing his influence.

We learned Rangers was losing between £200,000 and £300,000 a game in income. We desperately needed investment. The group being fronted by Dave King offered to invest £8 million. That would have helped us a great deal. It would also have encouraged the supporters to buy season tickets and come back to games in larger numbers.

We received information from London that a business associate of Mike Ashley was committed to underwriting a share issue in September. But shortly beforehand we were told he had withdrawn. There wasn't enough time for anybody else to step in and the offering wasn't a great success. In fact, it almost failed. You need 75 per cent uptake and it just got that and no more. They wanted to raise £4 million and only managed to bring in £3 million.

The biggest beneficiary of that was Mike Ashley. It put him in an ideal position to give Rangers loans. Within a week of that happening he went out and bought shares on the open market from institutional investors Hargreave Hale for £850,000. Instead of putting money into the club he chose to give it to a private investor.

Did Ashley ever want to own Rangers? Nobody will ever know. Did he want to control the retail division of the club? Of course he did. He has done that with numerous clubs in England. Every single business decision which was made after that was ultimately to his benefit.

A new company called Rangers Retail Ltd was incorporated in September and he was one of three directors. What it was for we will probably never know either. But we heard he was looking for a greater chunk of the business, the shirt sponsorship and to control the badges and the crests.

The club had to redo the deals when we accepted further

loans from Ashley even though there were offers of alternative investment from elsewhere.

The biggest concern I had was if Rangers International Football Club was to enter administration at some point further down the line would Rangers Retail Ltd in turn have to go into administration? If the answer to that question was no then if somebody was to come along and try to bail us out they would find there was no income from merchandise and shirt sponsorship and discover the badges and crest and the assets were also under the control of somebody else.

Rangers Retail Ltd was initially 51 per cent owned by Rangers and 49 per cent owned by Sports Direct. But that that changed to 25 per cent and 75 per cent when a £10 million loan was agreed in January.

Sons of Struth published that information and were told we were mad. More lawyers' letters came in. Strangely enough, they weren't about the accuracy of what we had stated. They were always concerned with the information being obtained illegally. Lo and behold, he gained control of the badges.

Everything we predicted came to fruition. We were always vindicated. But every time that happened it concerned something which was to the detriment of the football club. So there was no gloating on our part. We were just concerned at the seriousness of what was happening. Our club was at risk because of the ridiculous agreements we have signed.

You can't have a partnership where both partners don't make money. Mike Ashley and Sports Direct making a profit out of their involvement with Rangers isn't a problem whatsoever. It only becomes a concern when Rangers aren't making anything out of their involvement with Mike Ashley and Sports Direct. That was what happened.

We started telling people that Rangers were only making between £2 and £5 out of every shirt sold. Once again, people mocked us. But when the accounts for the six months to June 30, 2014, came out in November it transpired that Rangers had only made 75p for every £10 spent on official club merchandise.

Our understanding was that Crighton, Nash and Wallace were

keen to cut a deal with the group King was fronting. Now, Nash and Wallace were always keen to do that. But when Crighton changed sides and joined them it became obvious to Ashley he had to do something or he would lose all of his power in the boardroom.

Accepting the offer would have been the right thing for the club. But, once again, they did what was right for them. Towards the end of October it emerged that a £2 million loan, which was later increased to £3 million, from Mike Ashley had been accepted and that, as part of the agreement, Nash and Wallace would step down.

By all accounts, that happened when Crighton was on holiday. Pressure was apparently placed on Laxey Partners in their nominee's absence to accept the emergency funding. It was claimed the club was two days away from being put into administration and prospective administrators had been contacted by the club.

It was the first time since Sons of Struth was set up that directors had left and none of us were rejoicing. If they had been allowed to remain they would have been a bigger asset than they were under the old board. They were good people and good businessmen. I couldn't have said the same of many of the people they shared a boardroom with. In different circumstances, they may have been huge assets to the club.

Dave King, George Letham, Douglas Park, George Taylor and others had been prepared to put in the money up front. At one stage, the offer from King was £16 million of pure investment. That then changed to £8 million of investment and an £8 million loan.

But that was at the insistence of the board after discussions with Nash and Wallace. They felt that giving them £16 million of shares would impact on the existing stakeholders too greatly. So exactly how the deal broke down was changed so that the existing investors would be more likely to approve it.

But the supporters were told that 26 per cent of shareholders – the Mike Ashley and Sandy Easdale block which we came to describe as the Axis of Evil - would vote against it and it wouldn't be accepted. The club had to go out and borrow more money - and use its assets to do so.

We came to the conclusion that Sandy Easdale, through his proxy shareholding, was preventing outside investment from coming in and threatened to boycott games until he was removed.

By that stage, he had done so many things to anger the support. In September he was pictured on the front page of the Daily Record coming out of a restaurant in Glasgow city centre with Rafat Rizvi, a businessman who had been charged in Indonesia with corruption, money laundering and banking fraud and who was on Interpol's most-wanted list.

In an interview with STV the week before the Rangers AGM in December 2013, Easdale had denied having any involvement with him. He said:"No, I have not had any dealings with Rafat Rizvi."

The official explanation given after Easdale was spotted with Rizvi was he had no knowledge he would be present at the meeting with a prominent Malaysian businessman called Datuk Faizoull Bin Ahmad about a possible youth tie up with a club in Asia. I felt the club was once again treating the fans with absolute contempt, insulting their intelligence, with that account of events.

If a Malaysian football club wanted to set up a youth development system the last place they would go to get some pointers on how to proceed is, I was sad to say, Rangers. We had no scouting system to speak of, precious few coaching staff at that level and a disappointing record of bringing through decent young talents, Lewis Macleod aside. It made absolutely no sense. But that was what we were told.

Rizvi's involvement with the club is certainly murky to say the least. He was mentioned in the second leaflet Sons of Struth handed out. His name often crops up when Charles Green is mentioned and it is often suggested he is the man behind Blue Pitch Holdings and Margarita Funds Holding Trust.

Regardless of whether he was guilty of the accusations levelled against him, he was not the sort of character a fan would want associated with their club. For a director to be pictured with him after lunch at a city centre restaurant is embarrassing irrespective of what had been said before that.

But when the club accepted the Mike Ashley loan ahead of the offer of investment from the group led by Dave King, we decided to act. Boycotting your own football club is the biggest sacrifice you can make as a fan. I was also well aware that if we took that action and, God forbid, the club had gone into administration, we would have been blamed for it. In particular, I would have been the villain of the piece - despite the fact it was the inability of others to run a business which was responsible for the state the club was in.

I knew exactly how it would be spun. The snipers would have said: "Craig Houston and Sons of Struth told fans not to go to games. Because supporters stayed away we had no money and we had to go into administration. Our precious assets are now under the control of the man who has bailed us out of this mess."

But the harsh reality is the only way that you can influence the charlatans who run football clubs these days is to stop going. The Coventry City fans are a good example of this. They took the ultimate sacrifice and said: "No, we're not attending games." The owners threatened to put the club into administration. But, hat off to them, they got back into their own stadium. In certain circumstances it is the only action that will get a reaction.

We polled the Sons of Struth members. We put it to them : "Should we boycott?" And we asked them: "Should we boycott on a one match basis?" I was of the opinion that if we had called for an all-out boycott it would work against us. Thankfully, our members voted 50.1 per cent for a one game boycott while 49.9 per cent voted for the ultimate sanction.

We selected the next home game, a League Cup match against St. Johnstone in October, to stay away from. We had a protest outside the front door. Several hundred fans turned up to show their support and voice their dissatisfaction. It is impossible to say how many we persuaded to stay away from Ibrox that night. Not everybody who had decided not to attend was going to come and stand with us outside the ground. But the official attendance given was just 13,023.

From a personal point of view, that was the last time I went into the stadium when the old regime was in charge. I didn't make it public. I just stopped going. I had had enough.

Bizarrely, long before we decided to boycott the match, I had arranged for some friends who played for the Braehead Clan ice hockey team at the time to get complimentary tickets to that very same game. After the final whistle, I went to pick them up. We were heading into the city centre for a few beers. I got spotted by somebody and soon a story was circulating online that I had actually broken the boycott. I thought: "Are people more interested in Craig Houston than in fixing Rangers Football Club?"

I was contacted by telephone about a month later by a third party who asked me to call an out-and-out boycott. I outlined the reasons why I wasn't prepared to do that. As I have mentioned, I felt it would come back to bite us and reflect badly on the Sons of Struth as a group and me personally if another financial crisis arose.

The gentleman informed me: "It's alright. There's a group of wealthy Rangers supporters who will bail us out if that happens."

I said: "That's fine. Can you give me their names, their phone numbers and tell me how much money they're willing to pony up?"

I could guess who it was. But the individual declined to give me any names. They didn't want to stick their heads above the parapet. But they were quite happy for the buck to stop with me. I wanted to know as an insurance policy. I politely refused the offer. I couldn't agree to it. If it all went awry I knew I would be the one held responsible.

Many people have stated we brought the club to its knees so that Dave King could come in and take control. That is not the case. There are lots of things we could have done to accelerate that eventuality if it was what we wanted – which it wasn't – and we refused to do them. One of them was to call the boycott earlier. We could have done a lot of things differently if that was our ultimate objective.

We didn't take that step because of Dave King we took it because we felt it was the best thing for Rangers Football Club. We were never once asked to take any action for any one man, for Brian Kennedy, Dave King, Jim McColl, Paul Murray or anybody else. If they gained an advantage as a result of our protests and activities then so be it.

The personalities were irrelevant to us. We backed Dave King because we felt he was a better alternative to what was there. He was a supporter of considerable means who cared about the wellbeing of the club, not making a huge gain on his investment.

But if somebody else had come along who was a superior option they would have received our support.

NORMAN Crighton resigned as a non-executive director of Rangers at the start of December. He was effectively forced out. That proved there had been, as we had been saying for some time, a split in the boardroom. But it was far more important than that. It was arguably one of the key events in this whole saga.

It meant that Laxey Partners, the major shareholders who Crighton was appointed to the board to represent, had no control over the direction the club took. It was a hugely significant development.

The year before that Laxey had initially stated their intention to side with the fans and vote for the Requisitioners at the AGM. They ended up changing their minds and voting against them. But, slowly but surely, a split appeared and widened. The alliance fragmented as the financial position of the club worsened.

I instantly thought forcing Crighton and Laxey out was a huge mistake by the then members of the board and suspected then it may lead to their downfall. It was foolish, hubristic and short-sighted.

Something I have learned throughout this ordeal is that these people have complete confidence in their ability to come out on top in any situation. Sometimes that arrogance can be their undoing. It certainly was in this instance. I thought: "Big mistake. They've fallen out with the wrong people here."

Together, Mike Ashley, Sandy Easdale, along with his proxies, and Laxey Partners owned over 50 per cent of Rangers. They had complete control of the club. Crighton leaving changed that. It was a defining moment, possibly the defining moment, in the battle for power at Rangers.

The money people invest in and make out of Rangers is of no concern to me. Whether they make a profit or a loss is immaterial to me. They are viewing a football club purely as a commodity. It means much more than that to me and to a lot of other good people who care deeply and passionately about it.

But I was glad to see the back of Laxey Partners and their chairman Colin Kingsnorth because he was an unpredictable shareholder who, as we had seen the year before, would say one thing and spin 180 degrees and do another.

When Wallace and Nash departed, Derek Llambias, the former Newcastle United chief executive, and Barry Leach, the head of brands at Sports Direct, were brought in, initially as "consultants". They would soon become chief executive and finance director respectively.

It was obvious they were, despite the official line being spouted that they were the superior candidates for those roles, brought in primarily to represent the best interests of Mike Ashley and Sports Direct and not to serve Rangers. It was blatant.

David Somers, the chairman, later told the AGM that numerous candidates had been interviewed and Llambias and Leach were the outstanding applicants. But that, remember, came from a man who described James Easdale as "one of the best plc directors I have ever worked with in my life". He also said Rangers fans owed Brian Stockbridge "a debt of gratitude for holding the club together". So, understandably, nobody believed a word that was being said. They were Ashley's men. End of.

We had a lot of contact with fellow supporters groups in Newcastle. It started when the story about the naming rights to Ibrox being sold for £1 broke. They had lived through something very similar. Their stadium had been renamed a few years earlier. It changed from St. James' Park to the Sports Direct Arena. We had a lot of common ground and spoke to them frequently both online and in person.

They were far from complimentary about Llambias. They told us about the meetings they had had with him during his tenure at Newcastle when they were informed it would be far better for them if they didn't get angry. He was portrayed as, to be frank, a fairly unsavoury character.

When a picture of Llambias and Leach alongside Brian Stockbridge at the luxury Mar Hall Hotel just outside Bishopton was published on the front page of the Daily Record it did nothing to instil confidence in them. We were told by the club they had to meet to discuss contracts. Once again, nobody was buying that.

I had no dealings with either man. But I witnessed the pair of them in action at very close quarters during their time at Ibrox .

I saw supporters approach them to ask questions about Rangers first hand. The way they behaved towards them and conducted themselves made me utterly sick. The disdain fans were treated with by paid employees was absolutely appalling.

My mate and I went in to the Blythswood Hotel in Glasgow city centre for a drink one night and they were there. I was not of a mind to frequent an establishment with that sort of clientele. So I just used the toilet and left. But before I departed I saw Rangers supporters, in a perfectly calm and unthreatening manner, asking them questions. The replies they received revolted me. After a while Llambias and Leach called security. Nobody had been at risk as far as I could see.

I hadn't even been impressed with how they behaved before that. They were laughing and joking without a care in the world despite the predicament the club they were being handsomely paid to work at was in. The future of our club was in jeopardy because key commercial contracts were of benefit to Sports Direct instead of Rangers. I just looked on in utter disbelief.

I received a phone call a few days later from a news journalist at The Sunday Mail. He informed me Llambias and Leach had been threatened in the Blythswood Hotel and then suggested that violence had been used against them. The evening this was alleged to have happened was the same evening I had seen them being asked questions by fans in that establishment.

I got called up to Helen Street Police Station one day. Sandy Easdale had alleged I was attempting to put him and his brother James, whose house had been vandalised by that stage, in physical danger. He had a meeting with the police along with his lawyer Peter Watson and made that accusation. They clearly felt I was some kind of sinister figure who had turned the whole support against them and was planning to do them personal harm.

Up until that point, the regime in charge at the club had tried intimidation, they had tried legal threats, they had tried to bully newspapers into stopping speaking to us. None of that had worked. I felt that claiming we were threatening them was the last throw of the dice for them. But the police saw it for what it was. I got the feeling they were far from enamoured about having their time wasted on such nonsense. It was before James and Sandy

Easdale received death threats. That did happen later.

They got it into their heads I was behind it all and made a complaint about me. But I have no criminal record at all. Before I started Sons of Struth the only involvement with the police I had was handing in my driver's licence to get penalty points put on it.

THE Sons of Struth held another public meeting at the Hilton Grosvenor Hotel in October. We presented people with the facts about the stadium naming rights, about how Mike Ashley was trying to change the terms of contracts which were already onerous for the club and take a greater say in the day-to-day running of the club.

There were about 200 or 300 people there that night, John Brown joined us on stage. We asked those in attendance: "Is Sports Direct now a legitimate target for protests?" We had already agreed to do flash mobs – where a group of people gather at a specified time and place and perform an unusual act for a set period of time - outside of their stores. But we wanted to promote the idea to the wider fan base and get them involved. It had the desired impact. The 50 or 60 folk who later turned up at the stores were all at that meeting.

We turned up en masse at the Sports Direct store at The Fort in Glasgow one Saturday morning later that month. We had banners specially made up. Somebody had also produced cards which read: "Spivs Direct." There were photographers and journalists there. To create a visual image for their pictures we were asked to hold up £1 coins which we did. Those shots made it into a lot of Sunday and Monday newspapers. We then went in, filled out baskets and offered £1 for what we had picked up.

It was, I readily admit, all unbelievably childish. But, boy, did it generate good publicity for us and secure a hugely positive result. In the days leading up to that event, I was called by a representative of the police in Newcastle. He asked how many busloads of Rangers fans were turning up to protest in front of the Sports Direct stores there. The honest answer was none at all. It was just a wild rumour which had started circulating. But I allowed them to believe that was going to happen.

Sons of Struth did have smaller events going on at Sports Direct stores around the country. But it was just small groups here and there going into shops in ones and twos. There were probably only half a dozen stores targeted. The perception, though, among the company was this was going to happen all over. We were informed the company put on additional security in every single one of their stores as a result.

We had built up good contacts inside the Sports Direct empire and became aware those inside the security division of the company were, not to put too fine a point on it, keeching themselves in the run up to this. So much so, that they went to the police and put extra personnel on their doors. It was fine with us. We just let them think whatever they wanted to.

About a week before the protest was scheduled I was contacted by a third party – a Rangers fan who did business with Sports Direct and who I knew well – to find out exactly what we were planning. I told him I couldn't give him any information. I think that possibly resulted in all of the stories which were doing the rounds growing arms and legs.

In reality, we probably closed the tills in one Sports Direct shop for around an hour. But we caused havoc. People accused us of being immature and claimed we achieved nothing more than inconveniencing the staff on the shop floor. But none of the workers could have cared less. They got paid regardless of what we did. And it actually did work.

A few days before our planned flash mob protest a message from Sports Direct came back to me through the intermediary. I was asked: "What would it take for you to stand down on this?" The answer was simple. I said: "Give up the naming rights."

That is, eventually, what happened the following month. But Mike Ashley took his time about it. I don't think he wanted to appear to be getting pressurised by football supporters. Typically, he took something in return. He got 25 per cent of the trackside advertising at the stadium and control of the shirt sponsorship deal. It was a sweet deal for his company.

When Ashley handed back the naming rights, we speculated that he would have made up for it somewhere else. We were derided for saying that. But that is exactly what happened.

Sandy Easdale told a meeting of the official fans board in December that supporters "hadn't celebrated that enough". It was interesting reading the minutes of the meeting. Many of the questions which were being asked were things which Sons of Struth had been highlighting. That suggested to me we were having an influence.

Rangers announced the Ibrox club had made an £8.3 million loss in its annual accounts in November and set the date of the AGM for December 22. By that stage, the Sons of Struth campaign was starting to take a serious toll on me both physically and mentally.

One Saturday in the build-up to the AGM I had been out watching the football team I helped to coach in Houston in the morning and then the side my son played for in Hamilton in the afternoon. I had got soaked to the skin. That night I went to watch the Braehead Clan ice hockey team in what was not exactly the warmest environment to sit in for a couple of hours.

When I got home that night I switched on my iPad. The screen was blurred. I looked across at the television and it was exactly the same. I put it down to being dog tired. Not wanting to alarm anybody, I said goodnight and went to bed. But when I lay down and closed my eyes I saw different coloured flashing dots and started getting pins and needles in my arms and legs. I got up and called NHS 24 and explained what was happening to the lassie who answered the phone.

She told me to head to my nearest hospital straight away. The prospect of going to the Southern General at midnight on a Saturday wasn't an enticing one so I told her I would pop along the next morning. She said: "I'll send an ambulance. You're experiencing all the symptoms of a stroke." My father bundled me into a taxi and escorted me to hospital. Luckily, my eyesight returned to normal after an hour or so and they carried out tests until they were satisfied I was alright.

It gave me a real fright. I am convinced it was because of the stresses and strains of our campaign. I had been living for far too long on too little sleep. I think I realised at that point that I couldn't carry on the way I was for too much longer. But I couldn't back down by that stage either. I was in way too deep to do that.

CHAPTER 14

RETURN OF THE KING

"I am very angry about this total stupidity."

David Somers, Rangers chairman.

THE gazebo which was erected on the hallowed turf at Ibrox to shelter the Rangers directors, the "football board chairman" and their assorted legal advisors at the annual general meeting on Monday, December 14 , 2014, was a sorry sight.

It highlighted just where Rangers was at that moment in time. The AGM the year before had been a stormy occasion, as that one also turned out to be, but at least it was staged professionally and on a platform befitting an occasion of that type at a PLC company.

The tent was even held to the ground by containers full of water. It was depressing. I had seen more impressive sights in friends' back gardens at 50th birthday parties.

Some of the comments made by those at the top table that morning were scandalous. The one that rankled with me more than any other came from the Rangers chairman, David Somers. He told the assembled shareholders that questions would be taken two at a time. There was uproar when that was announced. Somers said: "When you get to be chairman of Rangers, you get to do it your way."

It was disgusting. It was a ploy he had used 12 months earlier which many of us believed was designed to prevent the individual who was asking the question from subsequently querying what he or she was being told. We were convinced it was done to stop there being any kind of meaningful dialogue.

We wanted there to be one question asked at a time as that meant whoever had the microphone was in control of the conversation. If they, not the top table, were happy with the response they received, then matters could proceed. If not, they could challenge it.

It wasn't an AGM full of shareholders. It was an AGM full of shareholders who were fans. I appreciate it must be difficult standing in front of so many people who are so hostile towards you. But the way thousands of supporters were spoken to that day was just reprehensible.

One thing which I found bizarre about the whole morning – and I made this point to Sandy Easdale further down the line as we spoke about how the Rangers support felt about him and his brother James – occurred after the meeting had concluded.

As the top table made their way off the pitch and into the stand to go back to Argyle House, one supporter broke from the crowd and went for them. Now, the object of his anger should really have been Somers for the shabby way he had conducted himself and addressed the fans that day. But instead he made a bee line for James and Sandy Easdale. Nothing came of it.

For me, that was a barometer of how the Rangers support felt about them. It displayed how they were viewed at that time. I got the distinct impression that Barry Leach, Derek Llambias and Somers were quite happy for the Easdale brothers to be the whipping boys at that juncture. I myself thought the flak would have been better directed elsewhere at that stage.

I noticed something else that day. There was only one steward on the running track and he was situated directly in front of where I was. All the other stewards were at the back of the stand. Apart, that is, from where I was. There was one at the end of the row I was on.

I may have been imagining it, but I am positive the way the security was arranged was intentional. It was as if they were intimidated. I must admit, maybe a small part of me wanted them to feel uncomfortable.

I had received a copy of an email from Somers to Justin Barnes, a lawyer acting on behalf of Sports Direct, from a very reliable source two days before the AGM. I was assured it hadn't been stolen or obtained by other illicit means. I had no doubts about its authenticity or reliability. The person who passed it on had provided me with information which had stood up on numerous occasions before that.

The email confirmed the board had been prepared to accept the offer of funding from Dave King and showed that Somers was concerned about losing his position – for which he was paid £60,000 a year to work two days a month – if it was.

This is what it said:

"Why have you changed yesterday's deal? Particularly for a particularly stupid alternative.

"Meanwhile I have received a formal proposal for a deal from Dave King and my board are clamouring for a board call to discuss it and no doubt approve it. A board on which James and I are in a minority.

"Dave King's proposal includes board seats, which means Sandy, James and I will not survive on this board very much longer. Yes, you can vote them off at the next AGM but they can do a great deal of damage before then.

"It we are going down this route because you guys are pratting about, then even I will be voting to put out a stock exchange announcement that we are terminating Sports Directs (sic) contract; even though it is one of the last board meetings Sandy and I attend.

"I am very angry about this total stupidity."

My initial reaction when I read it was one of complete shock. Here was a director showing he was more concerned with his own position than the future health of the club. He was practically begging Sports Direct to act and improve their offer so he could remain in place.

But when I re-read the email I realised it highlighted more. It showed the onerous contract with Sports Direct could be changed. Somers threatened them with that. It also proved three directors had been ready to accept the offer when two directors had publicly claimed it couldn't be accepted because they didn't have enough detail. It also said that Sandy Easdale wouldn't survive on the board. But Sandy wasn't on the board?

It was only a few paragraphs long. But it contained some staggering information. It revealed a lot of things which we had suspected and had been highlighting. We knew directors had been acting in their own interests and not those of the club. We knew there was support for the investment deal offered. Norman Crighton, Phillip Nash and Graham Wallace all ultimately lost their positions as a result of that.

I thought long and hard about what the best thing to do with the email was and decided to mention it in a question at the AGM. I felt the media would be able to report it more easily if a shareholder raised it. I was going to stand up and say: "You claim you turned down the offer of investment from Dave King because there wasn't enough information. So why do you say in this email which you sent to Mr Ashley's lawyers that the other three directors were prepared to accept it?"

Doing that would have allowed the media, who I was told were toiling to get their lawyers to give the green light to the story, to report it. I knew of at least two newspapers who had obtained it. But I wasn't allowed, either deliberately or due to the large number of irate fans wanting to vent their anger, to ask a question. So I returned home and put the leaked Somers email online.

The usual anti-Sons of Struth mob online accused me of making it up. They claimed it wasn't the work of the Rangers chairman because it read like a 10-year-old had written it. That made me chuckle.

But posting that email online was a defining moment for us. The number of messages I received from supporters after that telling me that they finally understood what we stood for and were trying to achieve was incredible. Some of them had been quite derogatory previously and actually apologised for what they had written. Most of those admissions were private, but many were public. That moment was when I felt we had the most backing from the fans.

Peter Watson, the lawyer who had been representing Sandy Easdale and who, as I have documented at length, I had been involved in a fair few exchanges with, was now acting on behalf of both Somers as an individual and Rangers as a football club. It was the first time I had been threatened by the club.

I received lawyers' letters after publishing that email. They didn't question the authenticity of it. They were more concerned with where it came from and the fact I had published the chairman's email address. As a result, I was actually able to contact the reporters who were chasing the story and confirm to them it was genuine. The Daily Telegraph and Daily Record soon ran it.

At no stage did anybody working on behalf of Rangers suggest the email was a fake. The charge levelled at me was that I had stolen it. But obviously you can't steal something that had been made up. So inadvertently they confirmed the missive was genuine. That actually enabled the mainstream media to run with the story.

The newspaper lawyers who had concerns about the email being concocted by some internet bampot used the threats against me to convince themselves it was genuine. If it hadn't been, the communications I received would have been of a different nature. All along I felt they were simply trying to ascertain who had leaked the email.

The only thing they were right about was that I had, unfortunately, not hidden Somers' email address when I had posted it online. I amended that quite quickly. He had actually told shareholders as he brought proceedings to a close at the AGM that if anybody had any further questions they should email him. But at one stage it looked like I was going to get arrested for publishing that.

It got as far as the police being called. They investigated it and I traipsed back up to Helen Street for questioning. It was suggested to me I had stolen the email by illegally hacking into an account or had published an email that had been obtained by that method. I was told there was a possibility I could be arrested. It was a worst case scenario. But they informed me that could potentially happen before the end of the week.

I understood the police needed to do their job. I knew they were obliged to investigate these accusations. But I must admit being told I could be arrested was quite frightening. Getting sued is one thing. Getting banged up is something else altogether. I don't mind admitting that it caused me a great deal of stress and worry.

Deep down, I knew I hadn't done anything wrong and had nothing whatsoever to worry about. I spoke to friends and they all assured me I would be fine. But crazy thoughts did go through my head. I did ask myself: "Am I going to be locked up for this?"

I said to the police officers questioning me: "It looks to me like they are just trying to find out the source of this leak?" I also told them: "I will categorically not tell you where this came from. I am not legally bound to answer it."

I was of the opinion that information was incredibly valuable to the Rangers support. I believed the individual responsible for it being made public had done us a massive service and deserved to have his identity protected. It would have been easy for me to give him up.

But that would have been unfair and wrong after what he had done to help us. If there were any repercussions arising out of me making it public I was quite prepared to accept them. The email was dynamite and the fans and shareholders deserved to know.

MIKE Ashley, the Newcastle United owner, came to an agreement with the SFA over his level of involvement with Rangers when he bought his 8.92 per cent stake in Rangers in 2012. It stipulated he would not be allowed to increase to 10 per cent or more due to his involvement with the English Premier League club.

But two years down the line he was trying to become the major shareholder in the business. He wanted to increase his stake to 29.9 per cent. The reason for that exact figure being if you buy 30 per cent of a company you have to make an offer to buy the rest of the company under takeover panel rules. It was important we nipped that in the bud and stopped him lending the club money. His position became stronger as the club owed him more money.

The Union of Fans got information to the SFA. We made sure they knew what the flipside of him being given the go-ahead to buy more shares was. We stressed the arrangement the two parties had should be honoured. We also explained what we believed had happened at the share issue in September, when the associate of Ashley who had promised to underwrite it withdrew just before it took place, and sat back and waited.

I'm not sure if any of that made any difference. But on Christmas Eve it was announced that the SFA had rejected a request from

Rangers for Ashley to increase his interest in the club to 29.9 per cent. I was surprised but relieved the governing body had stood their ground.

But Lewis Macleod, without doubt the best Rangers player at that time, was promptly sold to Brentford for a fee in the region of £850,000 at the end of December. The club didn't even wait for the January transfer window to open before flogging our star player. It soon emerged he had been offloaded for working capital and to secure another £500,000 emergency loan from Sandy Easdale.

By the way, Sandy Easdale didn't give us another £500,000 loan for nothing. It may well, as was made public at the time, have been interest free. But he received something in return. He got two seats in the directors' box for life to go along with the two he had been given by Charles Green the season before.

I am sure the Rangers fans would have put their hands in their pockets to keep the the club going if they had known what was in the offing. If Macleod had stayed until the end of the campaign he would, I am convinced of it, have been our Player of the Year. We may also have won promotion with him involved. His sale beggared belief. It was such bad business. How can you achieve best value for your top player before the transfer window has even opened?

Robert Sarver, the owner of the Phoenix Suns basketball team in the United States, made an £18 million offer for Rangers in January. I had been contacted by somebody close to the club a few weeks earlier telling me a foreign investor wanted to buy the club. Without informing me of who it was, I was told he would be the best thing ever.

Because of our recent history, I was cautious. We had been through hell after Craig Whyte and then Charles Green had taken over. Anybody who comes in to the club after that is going to be subjected to close scrutiny and be treated with scepticism. Anyway, it turned out to be Robert Sarver.

I met the person who got in touch with me on the morning of the AGM and was told the Sarver bid was about to be made public. I got the impression this gentleman believed it would help his associate's position if he had the backing of a prominent supporters group like Sons of Struth. I felt we were being set up to those ends.

I was quite sceptical. Robert Sarver owned a basketball team in Phoenix. Mike Ashley had a large business empire in the United States which was based in Phoenix. I was just uncomfortable with it for some reason. I am unsure whether he would have been good or bad for the club. I remained fairly non-committal.

I was neither pro-Robert Sarver or anti-Robert Sarver. I didn't think his bid would be successful. But I didn't want to be seen to be responsible for driving him away. Other supporters groups were subsequently invited to meet with the billionaire banker by the PR company he employed to represent him in Scotland. But I didn't receive that call. Nothing came of his interest.

At the end of January it was announced to the AIM Stock Exchange that an interest-free £10 million loan had been agreed with Sports Direct. It was secured on the Albion Car Park, Edmiston House, Murray Park and the registered trademarks. A further 26 per cent of the Rangers Retail Ltd was transferred.

The arrival of five loan signings from Newcastle at the end of the January transfer window stunk to high heaven. Gael Bigirimana, Shane Ferguson, Kevin Mbabu, Remie Streete and Haris Vuckic all came in early in February without manager Kenny McDowall, who by that stage had replaced Ally McCoist on a temporary basis, knowing anything about it. McDowall found out as he was watching Sky Sports News one day.

Vuckic was excellent and established himself as a first choice regular. But Bigiriman and Mbabu were never sighted, Ferguson only played briefly in two games and Street lasted less than a half. If Rangers had won promotion they would have been due Newcastle a £500,000 bonus.

I WAS as surprised as any Rangers fan when the news broke on New Year's Eve that George Letham, Douglas Park and George Taylor, wealthy supporters who had formed a consortium and were quickly nicknamed The Three Bears by the media, had bought 13 million 20p shares in the Ibrox club.

The Three Bears took their collective stake in the Ibrox club to

16 per cent and jointly became the biggest shareholder in the process. They bought out Laxey Partners, who had owned the largest single chunk of the company, for £2.7 million.

Colin Kingsnorth, the chairman and founding partner of Laxey, confirmed he had acted after Norman Crighton, his representative on the board, had been removed so that Mike Ashley was unable to take control of the club. I suspected something may be in the offing. But I received no inkling about what was going to happen. Nobody let on.

I had got to know George Letham very well. I had, despite working for so many years in the motor trade, not met Douglas Park. But I knew of him. He had a reputation as a shrewd businessman who ran a tight ship financially. I had also heard of George Taylor, who was a managing director with Morgan Stanley.

I got to know George Letham from going into Bar '72 at Ibrox on a regular basis. I would often bump into him on the terraces at away games. Initially, I didn't know he was so well off. He was just another Rangers fan to me. The first I knew he was a man of some means was when he had given the club a £1 million loan the year before. It was quite surreal when I realised it was him who had put up the money.

He was just a rank and file fan in my eyes. He is a great character. A lot of people with his sort of money are quite showy about it with the way they talk, act and dress. George is the opposite of that. He is a very humble bloke.

A lot of Rangers fans thought that was game, set and match. Some supporters were even determined to go out and buy season tickets at that stage. It was certainly an important moment. But we urged caution. All we had was some Rangers-minded individuals who had acquired a sizeable tranche of shares. We still held no sway in the boardroom. We were wary of what the regime would do to counteract this group buying shares.

Dave King had told Rangers supporters at the start of that year that he would rather buy fresh shares than existing shares so the money went into the club. But he had conceded that, if need be, he would change his approach if necessary.

His plan seemed sound. There would be a share issue, he would underwrite it, put millions of pounds into Rangers and the club would benefit from his investment. But, of course, he was prevented from putting any money in. Like so many supporters, I got frustrated when nothing happened. I kept asking myself: "When is Dave King going to buy these shares?"

But a few days after The Three Bears upped their stake he finally made his move. His company, New Oasis Investments Ltd, bought a total of 12 million shares owned by Artemis, Miton Group and River and Mercantile. He became the largest single shareholder with a stake of 14.7 per cent.

I had met and spoken to Dave King on several occasions. A hilarious situation occurred shortly after he had bought his shares when I was walking through Glasgow city centre to a meeting I had arranged at the Buchanan Galleries shopping centre. There was a guy walking alongside me in the same direction. I thought: "That looks like Dave King." He looked over and said: "Oh, hi Craig!" I said: "It is you!"

A guy who was worth tens if not hundreds of millions of pounds was walking around the city centre without a care. He had no security guards with him. He wasn't being ferried about in a chauffeur-driven limousine. He was just going about his business in a very ordinary way.

It turned out he was heading to a meeting just next to Sauchiehall Street so we walked together for a while and then stopped for a chat as we were about to go our separate ways. I said to him: "Dave, can we just get this thing over the line." We spoke for a few minutes and then headed off in opposite directions.

After my meeting I was heading down Buchanan Street and my mobile phone went. It was Sandy Easdale. He said: "Have you heard a rumour that Dave King is back in the United Kingdom?" I told him: "He's a bit closer than that Sandy. I've just seen him on Buchanan Street."

Things started to move quite quickly after those share purchases.

CHAPTER 15
RANGERS RENT-A-MOB

"For the avoidance of doubt and so that all Rangers fans are again reassured, the board has stated that it has no intention of granting security over Ibrox to anybody."

Statement on the official Rangers website.

ONE of the three main aims of Sons of Struth when we started was for Ibrox to be safeguarded. We never once lost sight of that objective.

STV broke the story in January that Rangers had lodged advance notices of security against Ibrox and Murray Park on behalf of Sports Direct with the Register of Scotland. That meant only that company could be granted security on the properties for a 35 day period.

It also made it impossible for the club to accept the conditions of a counteroffer from The Three Bears consortium, who had pledged to supply £5 million in return for security over Murray Park and two places on the board, to be accepted in that time.

That move was enough to tip the fans, even the ones who had been opposed to us from the start, over the edge and turn them against the board.

Sons of Struth had been saying for two years that using the stadium for security was the board's long game. We were ridiculed for that and told the board had put out a public statement confirming they would not do anything to that end. Indeed, they had released two statements to that end.

In May of 2014, they had said: "For the avoidance of doubt and so that all Rangers fans are again reassured, the board has stated that it has no intention of granting security over Ibrox to anybody."

Then two months later they claimed: "The board is happy to reaffirm its position, which has never been a matter of debate, by confirming once again that it will not enter into any form of sale, securitisation or leaseback of Ibrox Stadium."

We had already targeted the league game against Hearts on a Friday night in the middle of January for a protest. That match being played just a day after the plans to use the stadium as security for a loan became public ensured a huge turnout. We stressed we wanted all fans, irrespective of how they felt about Sons of Struth, to take part. It was the largest gathering we attracted before a game. The police estimated there were 5,000 supporters at it.

It emerged before kick-off in the Hearts game that Dave King had lodged paperwork calling for an extraordinary general meeting to remove all four directors, James Easdale, Barry Leach, Derek Llambias and David Somers, and install himself, John Gilligan and Paul Murray in their place.

About 30 or 40 of us set off from The District Bar on Paisley Road West that night and walked up to the stadium together. When we turned onto Edmiston Drive at the back of seven o'clock I was stunned at the size of the crowd and volume of the chanting.

That protest was very heated. At one stage the police had to call for reinforcements as the barrier at the front door was moved back by the front line. The fans were upset at what may have been about to happen to the stadium. They are passionate people and there was a lot of anger that night. But it was much ado about nothing.

My dad walked up to the game himself that night and I didn't see him until a good while afterwards. He was in his seventies and I expected him to be standing well to the back or the side of the crowd. But when I met up with him he told me:"I nearly got in!" I said:"What are you talking about?" He said:"When the fence went up I was right beside it"

He had been standing right at the front next to the hard core protesters. He said:"I just got carried away and stormed right to the front. I was really angry."When he got back to the house my mum was not best pleased with him. He had been on the BBC News looking like he was part of this unruly mob. For a pensioner to do something like that shows how strongly the ordinary supporter felt about the predicament.

The protests started 45 minutes before the game got underway and went on for 10 minutes after it kicked off. We were boycotting the games at that stage and only heard the game had been abandoned after just 25 minutes because of the heavy snow which had fallen as we were walking away from the ground.

There was an incident at the front door of Argyle House shortly after the game was brought to a premature end. I think it was fair to say that, because of the timing of it, those involved had been at the match.

A video was put up online afterwards which showed what happened. A group of kids had been shouting outside and had tried to enter. Liz, a member of staff had gone to put her hand over the door to stop them entering. It flew open and hit her in the face. She lost a tooth. It upset me that an employee could get hurt by a supporter in that way.

However, I still felt the reaction to it online was excessive. Essentially, half a dozen of the boys got in, danced around in the reception singing "sack the board" and unfurled a banner. The police then turned up and huckled them out. That was pretty much it.

As appalled as I was at the injury the employee sustained, what happened after that was a concern for me personally and underlined what was going on inside the club at the time. We had a lot of support from staff throughout our struggle. But it also became evident to us there were many people who worked there who disliked what we were doing intensely.

The first thing the security staff did when they spoke to Liz was say: "Was it Sons of Struth who did this?" She knew exactly who we were and informed them it wasn't us who were responsible. They seemed genuinely upset she wasn't willing to implicate us.

Some Rangers fans made some outrageous claims about Sons of Struth online afterwards. A couple of reporters called me about it. Fortunately, they saw the slurs for what they were, baseless attempts to blacken our name. No media outlet ran with the inaccurate version of events our detractors tried to peddle. Our protest finished just after the kick off. This happened about half an hour later and by that time we were in the pub.

A few stories I heard after that night didn't sit easily with me. We were told the official delegation from Hearts, including the new owner Ann Budge, had been quietly disgusted with what was being done and said inside by some of their Rangers counterparts in the Blue Room that evening. The television was turned up to drown out our chanting apparently and they were very dismissive of us. We were accused of being nutters.

But we weren't too shabby at organising protests and letting the board now what we thought of them. We had another couple after that, one before the Scottish Cup game against Raith Rovers a few weeks later and another at the SPFL Championship game against Hibs the week after that.

At the Raith Rovers game there were a couple of thousand fans outside. Because of what had happened at Argyle House after the Hearts game, we were really keen for nobody to disrupt it or misbehave.

The police asked us to stand 10 feet back from the barriers to prevent a repeat of the jostling at the front door. So I unfurled our Sons of Struth banners at that point and told people not to go in front of them. Just as I was doing that, one of the police officers called me over and pointed out a fan who was being a bit boisterous. So I went and stood behind him.

He was clearly under the influence of some substance or other. He was acting stupidly and shouting obscenities. I had a word with him and he moved to the side. But a couple of minutes later he came back, grabbed one of our flags and started all of his nonsense again. I went over and took the banner off him and told him to calm down.

There were a few incidents involving the same person. But we got to the end of the protest without any bother. At the end, as the fans started to disperse, the police officer came over and said: "The match commander saw what you were doing there and was really impressed with how you controlled the situation. We didn't have to get involved at all."

I found out later the individual had got into bother with the police after that and had been arrested. Ironically, his name turned out to be Craig Houston. I am sure that raised a few eyebrows when he was being checked in at the police station that night. I was surprised none of our adversaries picked up on it either. I was hoping somebody latched onto it.

The board stayed away from the Raith Rovers game. They put out a statement on the official website saying that "after advice from the club" they had not attended due to concerns over the safety of the "fans, stewards and staff". I felt it was an attempt to paint the protesters in a bad light and show they were whiter than white ahead of the EGM. The following week there was a far bigger crowd at the Hibs game and they were able to turn up at that. Go figure.

At the Hibs game we had former players John Brown, Iain Ferguson and Nacho Novo standing alongside us at the front door before kick-off. I didn't think they would turn up. But Bomber had been refused entry to the directors' box a few weeks before that and I think that incident had convinced him to get involved.

John had a long-standing request from a friend to take him to the directors' box. He knew Ally McCoist wasn't going to be at Rangers as manager forever so he arranged for him to leave a couple of tickets on the door. The club got wind of it, opened the envelope and McCoist was told an hour before kick-off they weren't getting in. The manager then had to send a text to his pal telling him what had happened.

Some decent people at our club managed to arrange for alternative tickets in a good area of the main stand. For him to be treated in that manner was very shabby. The guy had shed blood and broken bones for our club.

Gordon Dinnie of the Rangers Supporters' Trust got a hold of a rat mask before the Hearts game. The significance of that was that John had called the directors rats as he asked a question at the AGM. The fans had latched onto that in the aftermath and lots of pictures and logos began appearing online. Sons of Struth started using one as a profile picture on our Facebook page.

At the Hibs game I had arranged to meet Iain, John and Nacho at the John Greig statue and walk along to the front door. As I got there I could see Bomber with his back to the road. Before I got to him, I put the rat mask on and tapped him on the back. I said: "I'm wanting a word with you! What have you been saying about me and ma pals!" I got a look off him which I think a few wingers have seen over the years.

I said to him:"Let's walk up to the front door together and see what security do." But he got grabbed by fans looking for autographs and photographs as we made our way through the crowd and when I got there I was by myself. I said to the security guard: "Hello. I work here. Can I come in?" I got a round of applause for that and a few photographs taken with the mask on and a wad of notes I had in my pocket. It made a fair few papers and was on Sky Sports News.

THE minute King made his move and called an EGM I was confident he had more than 50 per cent of the Rangers shareholders behind him and would be able to finally oust the hated regime running our club. I didn't imagine for a second he would have taken such a dramatic course of action if he wasn't sure he would succeed.

Once again, a lot of fans were ready to celebrate at that stage. Once again, I believed they were getting a bit carried away. It was, I felt, all well and good having the necessary votes to win an EGM when you call it. It is having them on the day which is important.

I remembered only too well when The Requisitioners looked set to win a vote and get elected to the board two years earlier. They agreed not to call for an EGM in order to save the club money and instead ceded to holding the vote at the AGM. The board promptly went out and enlisted the support of Laxey Partners by allowing them to appoint a director and clung on to power.

I was pretty comfortable King, Murray, the former director who had been working away tirelessly to bring about change, and Gilligan, a one-time managing director of Tennent Caledonian Breweries and a lifelong Rangers supporter known to many fans, had the backing required when the EGM was called. But I remained cautious.

When the club finally announced the details of the EGM in February it highlighted many of the reasons why the supporters wanted the people in charge of Rangers out. Instead of just publishing the date, time and venue, they tried to smear the opposition and show how wonderful they were. It was not how a PLC company should be conducting itself in public.

Their 4,000 word statement outlined Derek Llambias's achievements in the game – including the sale of Andy Carroll from Newcastle United to Liverpool for £25 million. It was comedy gold. The striker was a pretty hot property in England at the time. All Llambias would have needed to do to facilitate that transfer when he was chief executive at St. James' Park was answer the telephone.

To our amazement, the Millennium Gloucester Hotel in London, not Ibrox Stadium in Govan, was chosen to host the EGM. It was very quickly alleged by people directly involved in the process that a campaign of disruption was being planned. We were told by good sources that a gang of yobs from London masquerading as Rangers fans were going to turn up and cause havoc at the hotel. We were told that by two completely separate sources. So we felt it was safe to conclude the threat was genuine.

By all accounts, this rent-a-mob was going to arrive dressed in Rangers t-shirts, strips and scarves, cause chaos both outside the hotel before the meeting and inside the hotel during it and force proceedings to be called off. We couldn't allow that to happen. We set our minds to counteracting it.

The Rangers supporters had played into their hands to an extent with our abusive conduct at the previous two AGMs. That was the reason given for holding the EGM in London. But it was claimed some people wanted a controlled environment where they could carefully orchestrate scenes of affray, abandon the meeting and give themselves another month to hatch their next ploy. We came to the conclusion that the only way to combat what they were planning was to make sure it did not take place in London.

We made it known in the media that we were planning to fill a convoy of buses full of fans and shareholders and drive down to the EGM so they could vote. We wanted to show that too many people would turn up and the hotel, which could only house 500, would be unable to accommodate them. We hoped the club would then be duty-bound to change where the meeting was being held.

National newspapers ran stories saying that we were laying on transport for shareholders from Ibrox Stadium to the Millennium Gloucester Hotel. The reality, though, was that nobody made a single call about booking a single bus. It was all just smoke and mirrors. But there was good reason for our duplicity. We had been informed there was a serious risk of that meeting being disrupted intentionally and abandoned and that would have bought the board even more time. They could not be trusted in those circumstances.

But the stories about busloads of Bears descending on this very plush establishment in Kensington had no immediate impact. So we started an e-petition. It was titled: "I am a Rangers supporter and shareholder and I am going to come to the EGM at the Millennium Gloucester Hotel in London." Within a few hours over 2,000 people had signed up to it.

We forwarded that to the club, the hotel, and the nominated advisor WH Ireland. We said: "Let's just change the venue now. Let's not wait until the day of the event for it to be called off due to too many people turning up." We didn't, of course, let on that we knew what was afoot.

The club eventually moved it after being told the venue was no longer available. But they just chose another hotel in London. The next location was the Grange Tower Bridge. We then faced a real quandary about what to do next. It was feasible they could have just kept moving it. It could have gone on forever. We started to discuss letting it go ahead as scheduled and sending down 50 to 100, shall we say, handy sorts to keep order and marshal the crowd.

But events took a strange turn due to some mischief making from our friends in the East End of Glasgow. The Grange Tower Bridge Hotel started getting bombarded by messages from Celtic fans on Twitter warning them of the anarchy which would ensue if they went ahead with the event.

I got in touch with the head office of the Grange Hotel Group when that happened. I said: "I think you've been the victims of a hoax here. This is just Celtic fans having a bit of fun."

The chap I spoke to was a football fan and accepted what I was telling him. I told him: "We want this EGM to take place. We don't want it cancelled. We want this EGM to go ahead and the board to be voted out. Why would Rangers fans jeopardise that? If you want any assurances about who I am then just Google my name or Google Sons of Struth."

We wanted to keep the arrangement as it was until we decided upon a course of action. We wanted to control the situation not fans of our fiercest rivals. The individual I spoke to assured me he would take on board my comments. But within an hour it was announced they had cancelled as well. That left everything up in the air once again.

Fortunately, the board then relented and confirmed the EGM would be held at Ibrox as it should have been in the first place. So Celtic fans were probably, inadvertently, responsible for the meeting going ahead and being held at the venue we wanted in the first place. I never did get round to thanking them for that.

I HAD started meeting Sandy Easdale on a fairly regular basis around this time. I had been approached by a Glasgow-born businessman who lived and worked in London. He told me he was confident he could lay his hands on £3 million at short notice and said if that money was ever needed to save Rangers I should get in contact with him and he would be more than willing to put it up.

Not surprisingly, that offer stuck in my head. Shortly after the EGM was called I had an idea. I immediately put it to him: "Why don't you buy Sandy Easdale's shares off him?" The bloke had actually thought of exactly the same thing himself and was very keen about the proposal.

I put out information on Facebook that a complaint had been made to the Financial Ombudsman about Sandy Easdale. Whether the accusation levelled against him was actually true or not was neither here nor there. All I did was post what had happened. It was confirmed to me by somebody inside Ibrox. It was a factual statement.

The next morning I received an email from a lawyer at Peter Watson's firm saying it was defamatory and untrue and asking me to remove it. I just ignored it. I didn't even bother replying.

But later that day I received an email from Peter Watson himself telling me I was breaking the law and outlining what was going to happen to me if I refused to take it down. I ignored that too.

Later that night I was sitting in my parents' house and the telephone rang. It was Sandy Easdale.

He said: "Hi Craig, it's your nemesis here. Gonna do us a favour? My lawyer's giving me a hard time about this thing you've posted online about me. Any chance you could take it down?"

"Aye, no problem Sandy, hold on a second and I'll go and get my laptop and take it down right away."

"Will you? Oh, that's great."

"Sandy, I'm kidding. Do you really think I'm going to do that? How would I benefit? I wouldn't. But you would. You'd get less grief from your lawyer. This is another example of him guiding you. I'm not interested. There's no point in me doing it."

"Aye, but if you do I'll not sue you?"

"Sandy, I'd love you to sue me over this. You wouldn't stand a chance of winning and it would be more bad publicity for you."

He then accused me of trying to act like a hard man because I was in a room with all of my mates. I was sitting with my mum and dad, two pensioners. I reminded him that he had phoned me. I said I would happily meet him at noon the next day in person and talk in exactly the same way mano-a-mano. He told me he would be at his garage down in Inchinnan and we agreed a time.

When I hung up I thought: "I've got absolutely no idea what I'm going to see him about?" So I contacted the businessman in London and asked if I could offer to buy his shares on his behalf. He was very keen and was prepared to pay over the asking price for them.

I was late getting there. Sandy must have thought I wasn't going to trap. When I was ushered into his office his face visibly dropped. He looked awful as we were walking through to his boardroom. He informed me he had received a lot of threats since the Hearts game. He said his secretary had even been getting abuse for not putting the calls through.

We sat and had a long conversation. I made it quite clear to him the game was up. I pointed out the existing board would be voted off, that he had between now and then to repair his damaged reputation and had to do something. I asked if he would sell his shares to me.We discussed it in some detail, the mechanics of how it would work, without ever actually naming a price.

But as time went on it dawned on me there was no point in him selling his shares because the EGM was won anyway.The only beneficiary would be Sandy Easdale who would save some face and receive more than he should have for his shares. Nevertheless, I still thought it would be beneficial to rid the club of him.

We had four meetings like that in the coming weeks. I informed him that I, who had probably been his most vociferous critic, would speak publicly and positively about his decision to the media if he agreed. I think he was a bit discombobulated that his greatest adversary was prepared to help him like that.

At one point in our discussions, he agreed that he would speak to a newspaper journalist and state he was going to vote for Gilligan, King and Murray at the EGM. He was cautious about going against Llambias and Leach so openly. But he decided to go public with his intentions.

An interview was arranged for a set time and day about a week before the EGM.The front page, back page and an inside spread in a national newspaper were set aside for the story.A journalist was lined up to go and speak to him.A photographer was organised to take a picture of him ticking the boxes on his voting card.

I was also primed to receive a phone call after the interview and give a fan's reaction. I was going to speak about his actions in glowing terms. It didn't sit right with me. I shouldn't have made the effort to be honest. But I was a man of my word so I was prepared to do it.

I was sitting in my motor in the car park at the Phoenix Centre in Linwood when my phone went. It was Sandy Easdale.

He said:"I think I might abstain from voting."

I told him:"But that'll mean you don't vote for your brother."

"I'll just abstain from voting for the proposed directors."

"Don't bother getting the journalist to phone me. I won't support it.That wasn't our agreement."

That was the last time I ever spoke to him. On the day of the EGM he abstained from voting completely.

During our talks, Sandy Easdale seemed convinced he could stay and work with the new board. He appeared genuinely mystified why he would have to move on. He just had no grasp of what the public perception of him was. It beggared belief. How could you see the protests we had held and read the stories in the newspapers and still think you could have any sort of role at the club going forward?

At those meetings we spoke about him selling his shares and backing Gilligan, King and Murray at the EGM. But something else cropped up too. As we spoke, I told him we needed to get a new manager in and to get the team playing better football ahead of the Premiership play-offs if we were going to win promotion back to the top flight.

By that stage Ally McCoist had resigned and been put on gardening leave and his assistant Kenny McDowall had taken over on a temporary basis.

I said: "The team is playing shite! What does the football board actually do? Go out and get us a new manager!"

He asked me who I would like to see appointed. I gave him two names. He said: "I like the first name?"

I told him: "Well, I know him. I've spoken to him on numerous occasions about Rangers. He'll take the job if he's offered it."

He asked if I could phone him up and sound him out. So I did exactly that. The first thing the chap said to me was: "Hold on a minute! You don't like these guys!"

I responded: "I know, but this is about the future wellbeing of Rangers."

He was, as I had predicted, agreeable to a potential approach. He was confident he could do a job despite the difficult circumstances and get the club promoted. I know his appointment would have been warmly welcomed by the overwhelmingly majority of the supporters

I then passed on his agent's details to Sandy Easdale. He didn't phone him. If he had done and this fellow had been brought in as manager then it would have been beneficial for both him and the club. But nothing happened. As was the case in so many things he did, or in this instance didn't do, it really rankled me.

CHAPTER 16
NEPHEW OF STRUTH

"You've played some game son."

Walter Smith, former Rangers manager.

DESPITE the venue of the EGM being moved from the Grange Tower Hotel in London to Ibrox, we couldn't dismiss the possibility that the rent-a-mob we had been warned about would still turn up and disrupt proceedings.

So, unbeknown to a lot of folk, we had people, rank-and-file fans, friends of Sons of Struth, placed at strategic points in and around the stadium on the day of the meeting specifically looking out for any signs of disorder.

There were three routes in to the Copland Road Stand. I had people with mobile phones posted at different points on all of them to alert us to anything we should be concerned about. They were told to let us know if any unusual groups appeared so we could somehow prevent them from gaining access to the stadium.

But we were confident nothing was going to happen. By that point, James Easdale, the non-executive director, had gone and David Somers, the chairman, had resigned. It looked as if Derek Llambias, the chief executive, and Barry Leach, the finance director, knew it was over for them. But we took precautions just to make sure.

A few supporters had been invited to a meeting with John Gilligan and Paul Murray before it and I asked them how much support they needed to receive from Rangers fans, who held between 16 and 18 per cent of the shares, to get in. The answer was straightforward. None. They had the backing they needed from the investors.

They told us they called the EGM when they knew they had over 50 per cent of the votes they needed and then went looking for more support. John said: "In football terms, we're leading 3-0 going into time added on – but we're still looking for a fourth goal."

BuyRangers and Rangers First, the two fan ownership groups, polled their members on which way they should vote. The results showed between 96 to 98 per cent wanted to remove the old board and install a new board. I thought it was important the fans, not just the major shareholders and institutional investors, were involved in the whole thing. It meant they felt part of it.

I think it is fair to say that, as thousands of fans had taken part in the polls, that is how supporters felt at that time. It actually scares you how active and noisy the tiny minority who were supportive of the board were online throughout our struggle. They made their group appear far larger than it actually was. They told us we didn't speak for the majority. Well, it turned out we did.

Together, Dave King, The Three Bears, who are all effectively supporters, along with the Rangers fans, owned over 50 per cent of the club. Through the actions of a lot of people, protesting, boycotting, buying shares, we had managed to get into a position where the supporters actually did own the club. That meant the future was effectively in our own hands.

We had waited until the date of the EGM was set and the relevant paperwork was sent out to shareholders before we started asking for them to proxy their votes to us. As far as I was concerned, the main thing was that votes were proxied. Whether it was to BuyRangers, Rangers First or the Sons of Struth, it didn't bother me.

But it became a bit of a competition between the two fan ownership groups. They had, it seemed to me, been trying to outdo each other when it came to attracting members and buying shares in the club, for some time. Once the EGM was announced that changed and they became hell bent on getting the largest number of shares and percentage of the vote, proxied to them.

The Louden Tavern Ibrox arranged for fans to go down with their proxies before a game and give them to either Rangers First or the Rangers Supporters Trust. It was quite a weird sight. When you went in you were asked who you wanted to proxy your shares to.

Then you were directed to where that group was. Rangers First was in the bar. The Rangers Supporters Trust was in the lounge.

I felt that was symbolic. It showed a divide that existed in the support. It was disappointing. To me, it wasn't about which group got the most. The way I saw it, we were all going to vote the same way anyway.

Sons of Struth agreed with The District Bar to use their premises as a drop-off or postal point for proxies. But we specified you could leave them for any group. You just had to state on the card who you wanted your vote to go to. We would ensure it was then passed on to them. It didn't matter who received the vote. What mattered was simply winning the EGM.

The District Bar became my local during our campaign. Many people I spoke to online drank in there and we ended up using it as a meeting place. The owner is David Currie, who is good friends with Ian Durrant, who pops quite a lot when he is passing, and is well known to supporters. We went in to The Grapes Bar as well. The staff and the regulars in both establishments were very supportive of what we were trying to achieve.

On the actual day of the EGM, I made the decision just to walk along to the stadium by myself to gather my thoughts about what we had finally achieved. I had been to the Fernando Ricksen tribute match the month before. But, that aside, it was the first time I had been to Ibrox since October. It was a strange day.

The meeting lasted 11 minutes. There was a nice atmosphere. Ally McCoist came in late on and got a warm round of applause. He sat just behind me. After it was all over I went up to him, shook his hand and asked: "You have voted the right way now haven't you Ally?" He said: "I'm sure you won't be disappointed Craig."

When I came out of the ground there were a lot of people milling about. A sporadic round of applause started. I looked behind me expecting to see Dave King or John Gilligan or Paul Murray. But none of them were there. The clapping was for Craig Houston. It was bizarre and quite humbling. There was a real lump in my throat I must admit.

I got a lovely text off George Letham after the EGM thanking me for my efforts. I, and every other Rangers fan, had a million reasons to thank him. I received a lot of messages. But that one really struck me. I thought: "Hold on! This guy gave the club £1 million to keep it afloat! And he's thanking me!" It was a measure of the man.

We knew it would be a few hours before the announcement was made official. I hung about for a bit and did a few interviews. I went down to The Louden Tavern for a pint and then made my way to The District Bar to wait for the result to come out.

Billy Montgomery came up and tapped me on the shoulder. He pointed out an elderly gentleman sitting at the end of the bar and said: "He's wanting a word with you." Truth be told, I was a bit irked because the result was going to come through any minute. But I didn't want to be disrespectful so I went over and introduced myself.

He shook my hand and said: "My name is James Struth. Bill Struth was my uncle. I want to thank you for all your efforts for Rangers." As God is my witness, as soon as the words left his mouth a huge roar went up. The result of the vote had gone up on the television and we had won by a huge margin. Gilligan, King and Murray had received around 85 per cent of the votes cast and had been installed as directors.

In the build-up to the EGM a strange thought had kept popping into my head for some reason. I was repeatedly asking myself: "I wonder who I'll be with when the announcement is made?" It was spooky that I was standing with a direct descendent of the man who I had named our organisation after.

James started telling me stories about his uncle which, I am now ashamed to admit, I actually can't recall. I was just so overcome by what had happened after two years of struggle and how surreal the situation was.

When I had regained my composure, I said: "James, I didn't put a great deal of thought into the name, Sons of Struth. I just thought your uncle stood for a lot of good things about our club and obviously the initials were SOS. If I've done or said anything you or your family didn't like can I just apologise to you. It was never my intention."

He replied: "Craig, I've never felt anything other than pride in anything you have done or said. It has all been for the betterment of Rangers Football Club." I was stunned. There was a lot of hurtful abuse thrown at me for using the name Struth. To hear a member of his own family, somebody who knew the man, give me his endorsement was wonderful.

Kenny McIntyre of BBC Scotland had called me up asking to do an interview and I had agreed to go into their studios at six o'clock that night. But I had inevitably ended up heading on to a few pubs to celebrate after the result was announced.

At one point, Monty said: "Aren't you meant to be on the radio? It's half past five!" By that point I was absolutely blazing. But I got bundled into a car and driven up to Pacific Quay. I can't remember anything about the show. The next morning I got a phone call from John Gilligan, the new director, thanking me for my work and telling me how well I had spoken on the radio that night. I didn't have the heart to tell him I was under the influence at the time.

Wee James, who sits in the wheelchair section of the stadium and who I had become friendly with along with his mother and his stepfather Heather and Deke Johnston, was having a firework display in his back garden to celebrate the result so I popped along there for a while. After that I went to The District Bar and had a brilliant night. Gillian had collected me from the station, taken me to James's firework display and dropped me at the District. She couldn't believe how drunk I was when I was collected from the BBC building.

My friends Scott and Stewart Campbell were there along with Davie Adams, another old pal from Linwood. So, too, was John MacDonald, the former Rangers player who 30 years earlier Scott, Stewart and I had gone to see as boys. We had become friends on Facebook during our campaign and I had spoken to him on several occasions online. It was nice to see him.

I HAD always said that all I ever wanted in return for what we did was for my father to get a seat in the directors' box at Ibrox for one Rangers game. On the Sunday after the EGM I got a phone call from the new director Paul Murray inviting me to be a guest at the game against Queen of the South with my dad. Somebody must have let him know that was important to me.

It was a fantastic night. There were a lot of friends and well-known faces. At one point Walter Smith came over to me in the Blue Room, grabbed my hand and said: "Craig, you've played some game son!" I was so honoured.

Dave King also made a point of speaking to me. He said: "Craig, I've not had a chance to speak to you, but thanks very much for all of your help and everything you've done in the last couple years."

I introduced him to my dad and he said: "You should be very proud of your son for all the work he's done and the effort he's put in. Not only has he fought for longer than most of us he's actually led us during this."

I was quite touched that a guy who has invested millions of pounds in the club should speak like that. A lot of people with Dave King's sort of wealth let it go to their heads. But he isn't like that at all. I have always found him to be down to earth, grounded, humble and a straight-talker. You can see the Castlemilk in him when you meet him.

John Greig, who had only been back at Ibrox once, when the Govan Stand was named in honour of Sandy Jardine, since resigning from the board during the Craig Whyte era, returned that night. He came over at one point and I asked him: "How does it feel being back? It must be very emotional?" He said: "Aye, son, but to be honest with you, there's a lot of faces in here I don't recognise." I said: "Oh, I'm very sorry, I'm Craig Houston from the Sons of Struth." He said: "I wasn't talking about you. Everyone knows who you are." It was absolutely mind blowing.

Most importantly, though, my dad had a great time. The highlight for him was getting his half-time pie in the Blue Room. He told me they were the best he had ever tasted. When the second half kicked off he stuck his hand in his pocket, pulled another one out and started eating it. I said: "Da! You're no' sitting in Section J any more!"

A BY-PRODUCT of what has happened at Rangers over the last few years is that the support now questions every bit of information given to them. We analyse and dissect every claim. Are we striking a deal with Nike worth tens of millions of pounds? Are we doing a tie-in with the Dallas Cowboys? Is this guy a multi-millionaire with wealth off the radar? Nothing is taken for granted.

Whoever turns up at Ibrox from now on will need to be totally transparent about everything they do and back up everything they say they are going to do before they get the backing of the supporters. It is no bad thing at all. If we had done that during the reigns of Sir David Murray, Craig Whyte and Charles Green then maybe things would have been different.

A Rangers fan sent me a lovely message a while ago. He wrote: "The board aren't the custodians of Rangers Football Club any more. People like Sons of Struth are. Where would we be without you guys? How much worse would things have got if you had not done what you did?"

I disagreed with what he said. I come from a sales background. If you set a target of selling 20 units in a month and you only sell 15 then, for me, you have failed in your objective. The Sons of Struth set out with three main objectives, to safeguard Ibrox, to get a board of directors we could be proud of and to have a clean set of audited accounts. Not all of them had been achieved.

A lot of people told me: "If it wasn't for Sons of Struth this guy or that guy would still be here." Somebody said something to me one day that I did actually agree with. He said: "You might not think you have made a difference, but where would the club be if you hadn't done what you have done?" I accept that. These guys may still be there. They could be ripping the club to bits.

When Graham Wallace took over as Rangers chief executive and produced his 120 day review he confirmed his predecessors made a mess of it with their onerous contracts and unprofessional practices. So perhaps we did help. But how much I don't know.

Dave King, Paul Murray and John Gilligan all stated at the press conference after they had taken power at the EGM that if it hadn't been for the people refusing to buy season tickets and staying away from games they wouldn't have got to where they were. What we did evidently helped the result.

I think the biggest thing that we achieved and can take some credit for is making the wider fan base aware of the serious mismanagement that was going on at Rangers. Years from now, somebody far cleverer than me will find out where the money all disappeared to, how it came out of the club and who pocketed it. All I know is that it happened. If anybody was stupid enough to believe the club wasn't being pilfered and raped then they were sorely mistaken.

We stood up and said: "These people aren't very good. In fact, these people are rotten. These people aren't working in the best interests of this club." We were told: "What do you know about it? Where is your proof? How can you say these things?" Unfortunately for us, the individuals involved were adept at concealing the evidence.

Of course, we were vindicated in due course. The 120 day review of company business that Graham Wallace carried out when he took over as chief executive showed that numerous "onerous contracts" had been struck during their brief but catastrophic tenure.

The impression I got was that the Charles Greens, Imran Ahmeds, Brian Stockbridges genuinely thought they were the cleverest people in the world. They believed they were more intellectual and more powerful than anybody else and than they actually were.

None of these people ever understood that we were there before them and we will be there long after them. They could not win. Rangers fans were always going to win because we will be here for eternity. We were fighting for something we believed in and loved. They were only here for a fast buck, to get a few photographs of the queen in their back pockets.

Bill Struth himself once said: "No matter the days of anxiety that come our way, we shall emerge stronger because of the trials to be overcome. That has been the philosophy of the Rangers since the days of the gallant pioneers."

I promised the thousands of Rangers fans who had joined Sons of Struth on the protest march to Ibrox that we would, one day, win. Thank God I was right.

ACKNOWLEDGEMENTS

TO thank all of the individuals who helped Sons of Struth would require a book in itself. Every single Rangers fan who held up a red or a blue card, chanted "sack the board", joined us on a march, withheld their season ticket money or turned up at a protest aided our cause. These supporters numbered tens of thousands. Without them, our voice would only have been a whisper.

Sandy Chugg is as close as I will ever have to a brother. I lost count of the number of occasions we argued and fell out during our campaign. Together we shared some incredible highs and some terrible lows. But our friendship is stronger because of all we have been through together.

Sandy was, due his grief at losing his own brother Christopher, sometimes unable to devote as much time to Sons of Struth as he would have desired. He had, though, a happy knack of reappearing just when I needed him the most. He introduced me to people who became of massive importance to our cause. He opened doors which may otherwise have remained closed. I would have been unable to do it without him.

The same goes for Big Boris and Billy Montgomery. It was not for nothing that I christened the pair of them "my verbal Valium". On many occasions, their timely phone calls and moral support brought me back from some dark places. I will forever be in their debt.

Gillian came into my life when I needed her the most. She has an uncanny ability to read situations and determine the reasons for somebody's actions in ways which I am, try as I might, unable to. I dread to think where I would be without her. LYL.

My mum and dad put a roof over my head when I became homeless and had no income. They also suffered and bore the brunt of my frustrations as the stress on me became unbearable. I was glad my dad saw that our struggle had not been in vain and also enjoyed that unforgettable night in the directors' box at Ibrox before he left us. He passed away peacefully in a hospital bed overlooking the stadium on the planned release date of this book. He was a husband, a father, a grandfather and my hero.

John Brown, Iain Ferguson, Richard Gough, John MacDonald, Michael Mols, Marco Negri, Nacho Novo, Alex Rae and Bobby Russell all backed Sons of Struth. To have Rangers players who you cheered on over the years stand shoulder to shoulder with you was an honour. They deserve

enormous credit for standing up and being counted when their club needed them.

Gordon and Clare McLennan, Les Henderson, Michael Grover, William Munro and Steven Cochrane were with Sons of Struth from the very beginning. I don't think they missed a chance to hand out leaflets before matches or hold up banners during games. Gordon's computer skills came in handy on numerous occasions. They are a great bunch who will be my pals forever.

Andy Smillie is a larger-than-life Bear who is known to many in our support. He is the kind of guy who wouldn't want me to divulge the full extent of his assistance. But those involved in Sons of Struth all know the amount he helped and will always be grateful. The timing of his interventions were extraordinary. He is a legend in my eyes.

Section J of the Main Stand has its own Sons of Struth supporters club. Alison and Thomas Ross, Barry France and Stuart McGill could always be relied upon to offer a much-needed word of encouragement and support. Alison's mother Nan Laurie is a wonderful lady who reminds me so much of my own gran and I always love bumping in to her at Ibrox. There are many other members of Section SOS who have given us so much.

Gary Simba, Dougie the Dug, Peter, S, Albertz, Gizzy and Kenzie all helped ferry me to and from away games and would help swell our numbers at our many protests. They are great lads who made many of the away days more enjoyable than the football.

Andy McLintock and Malcolm Murray spent endless hours on the telephone answering my endless questions about City of London rules and regulations as I strove to make sense of the manoeuvring by the Rangers board. Their expert knowledge was invaluable.

Harry, Jo, Debbie, Lindsay and big Craig are all part of the same family and they made me feel like another member of it with their words and generosity. Harry was the same age as my father. But he can often be seen standing on the terraces of sitting in stands dressed in his Hugo Boss jumpers and Stone Island jackets. This led to him being christened the "Inter City Pensioner". A lovely man and a lovely family. They helped me more than they can imagine.

Jean McGregor would pop up at everything we did. She was very supportive. I would always get a wee cuddle off her whenever we bumped in to each other. She embarrassed me once by slipping what I thought was a £10 note in to my jacket pocket "for your holiday". When I got home I emptied my pocket and it was a few quid more than I had thought. My daughter Amy got to swim with dolphins as a result. A diamond of a lady.

Gordon Dinnie, Christine Sommerville, Iain Paton, Derek Johnston and latterly Chris Graham are all members of the Rangers Supporters Trust committee. The support they gave me and Sons of Struth was great. Respect to all of them.

Ricki Neill of Rangers First was a latecomer to the scene. But his friendship was very welcome. The RST and RF continue to attract fans to buy shares in the club and should both be applauded for their efforts.

The Union Bears and The Blue Order are the two supporters groups who add to the noise and atmosphere at Ibrox. Both organisations helped enormously with the planning of our protests. Their advice was always invaluable. I am unable to name those who gave us their help. But they know who they are and so do I.

Kerry Coyne helped a lot in setting up our Twitter account in the early days. She was always willing to help and was only ever a phone call away.

Sie Leslie runs many Rangers nights and organises a lot of Q & A sessions with former players. He was forever willing to lend a hand and helped to put us in touch with some former players. Along with Gordon McLennan, he not only set up the Rangers Fans Forum meeting with The Requisitioners he also make it available live via the internet.

Mark Dingwall runs the largest Rangers supporters website Follow Follow. He is a seasoned campaigner and provided me with a wealth of advice and support.

When you get Mark on board you also get his good mucker David Leggat. Auld Leggo was like an uncle to me at times. A former journalist, author and blogger, he advised on media matters and lifted spirits.

Tam Green, James Riddell, David McCuthcheon, Drew Roberton and Andy Kerr all served on various supporters organisations. Getting to know all five of them has been a privilege.

The District Bar, The Grapes Bar and The Louden Tavern, Ibrox, all allowed us to use their premises for meetings. District owner Davie Currie and I became good friends. His wife Margaret, son Justin, daughter Gillian and the pub staff were always welcoming. I have known Robert Marshall at the Louden for a long time. But I became friendly with his wife Alice and son Greg thanks to the Sons of Struth campaign. Smiddy, his family and staff at The Grapes were also great with us.

These three publicans knew not all of the Rangers fans agreed with SOS. So to allow us use of their premises for meetings, drop off points for proxy votes and as gathering points for marches was much appreciated.

My old Linwood pals Scott and Stewart Campbell, David Adam, Bob McCarron, Del Whittington and Peter Watson (not the lawyer) were huge helps. Gavin McCallum roped me in to helping out with coaching at Houston FC (named after the Renfrewshire town). This was a welcome release for just a few hours a week. The kids, coaches and parents all encouraged me with my endeavours - even though not all of them were fans.

Gavin also introduced me and my daughter Amy to the Braehead Clan ice hockey team which proved another release away from the pressures of SOS.

Ian McColl and Gordon Bell from the Founders Trail not only educated me on Bill Struth but also supported many of our activities. I would recommend their trips to every Blue Nose.

Billy Morrison was able to show that I was related to William Wilton, the first ever manager of Rangers, after seeing a picture of his grave which showed that his wife's name had been Houston. He was good enough to spend several days researching the link. It is one of the greatest gifts I have ever received.

The Ballieston True Blues and Bridgeton Loyal RSC are among many supporters clubs who supported us throughout. Jim Clark from the Fergie Loyal, Eann Munro from the Granite City Rangers, Michael Munro in Cyprus, Kenny Park in Lanzarote, Mark Campbell, Mick Johnstone and John Campbell from The Gallant

Pioneer pub, the Blackpool True Blues, the London Branch of the RSC, the Bawdeep Phucket Loyal and Hong Kong RSC who even sent their banner for one of our marches.

Drumsagard Football Academy and the Drumsagard Loyal RSC were both a big part of my life for a while years before Sons of Struth was formed. The coaches and parents from the football academy and the office bearers and punters on the supporters' bus often helped us and sent words of support via text or on social media. Craig Queen, Brian Miller, Graeme Ireland, Tam Ross, Russell Main, Millsy, Tam McConnell, big Hutchy, Derek Reid and his daughter Carla, and Davie Miller, Halfway's very own Hugh Hefner, all encouraged me

Newspaper, television and radio journalists often incur the wrath of Rangers supporters just for reporting a story. I have discovered during the course of this process that most are simply doing their job. Indeed, we gained many a back page splash not to mention hours of television exposure and radio air time thanks to hacks who believed in our cause.

Dave King, Paul Murray, John Gilligan, John Bennett and James Blair were all, before their appointments to the Rangers board, known to me. Every one of them showed me courtesy, friendship and afforded me their time.

But the thousands of Rangers who supported Sons of Struth throughout our campaign deserve the most credit. We would have achieved nothing without them. It was a team effort. The chant at Ibrox has always been "we are the people!" We bloody well showed them that we are.

BIBLIOGRAPHY

Books
Rangers: The Complete Record, by Bob Ferrier and Robert McElroy, Breedon Books Publishing.

Rangers: An Illustrated History by Rab McWilliam, Aurum Press.

Web
Statement – Rangers Football Club official website, May 6, 2014

Rangers appoint Easdale to board as Murray and Cartmell step down, STV website, July 9, 2013.

Rangers: Craig Mather hires PR guru Jack Irvine, Scotland on Sunday, August 25, 2013.

Cops probe bigot attack on dog: yobs boot Celt pooch on head and call her a "Fenian", The Scottish Sun, September 12, 2013.

Shareholders claim Rangers' broker blocked compromise agreement with current directors, The Herald, Friday, September 13, 2013.

Club statement, Rangers Football Club official website, September 27, 2013.

Rangers: Mather discusses club future with Dave King by Alasdair Lamont, BBC Sport website, October 7, 2013.

Rangers made to delay annual meeting after court defeat, BBC Sport website, October 14, 2013.

Rangers: Murray calls for free vote on board appointments, BBC Sport website, October 15, 2013

Rangers chief executive Craig Mather resigns with Bryan Smart, BBC Sport website, October 16, 2013.

Rangers chairman David Somers says the majority of fans trust the Ibrox board, The Daily Record, December 21, 2013.

Rangers finances are fragile warns shareholder Sandy Easdale, by Alasdair Lamont, BBC Sport website, April 24, 2014.

Lewis Macleod: Brentford sign Rangers midfielder - BBC Sport website, December 31, 2014.

Rangers: Consortium buys 16% of club from Laxey Partners, by Chris McLaughlin, BBC Sport website, December 31, 2014.

Rangers: Lewis Macleod sale serves working capital needs, BBC Sport website, January 2, 2015.

Dave King takes 15% stake in Rangers as battle for Ibrox hots up, The Herald, January 2, 2015.

Rangers reject Robert Sarver's £18m approach for the club, BBC Sport website, January 6, 2015.

Mike Ashley posts intent to take out security on Rangers' Ibrox Stadium, by Grant Russell, STV website, January 15, 2015.

Dave King calls for Rangers EGM after Mike Ashley's swoop for Ibrox, by Grant Russell, STV website, January 16, 2015.

Mike Ashley tightens grip on Rangers with £10m loan, Daily Telegraph, January 27, 2015.

McDowall: I found out Rangers were signing five Newcastle players from Sky, by Gary Keown, The Herald, February 6, 2015.

Club statement, Rangers Football Club official website, February 8, 2015.

Rangers Fans Board Meeting Minutes, The Copland Road Organisation website, February 16, 2015.

Rangers will have to pay Newcastle £500,000 if they are promoted, by Luke Edwards, Daily Telegraph, March 31, 2015.